When Others Care for Your Child

By the Editors of Time-Life Books

Alexandria, Virginia

TIME®
LIFE
BOOKS

Time-Life Books Inc.
is a wholly owned subsidiary of

Time Incorporated

FOUNDER: Henry R. Luce 1898-1967

Editor-in-Chief: Henry Anatole Grunwald
Chairman and Chief Executive Officer:
J. Richard Munro
President and Chief Operating Officer:
N. J. Nicholas Jr.
Chairman of the Executive Committee:
Ralph P. Davidson
Corporate Editor: Ray Cave
Executive Vice President, Books: Kelso F. Sutton
Vice President, Books: George Artandi

Time-Life Books Inc.

EDITOR: George Constable
Director of Design: Louis Klein
Director of Editorial Resources: Phyllis K. Wise
Acting Text Director: Ellen Phillips
Editorial Board: Russell B. Adams Jr., Dale M.
Brown, Roberta Conlan, Thomas H. Flaherty, Lee
Hassig, Donia Ann Steele, Rosalind Stubenberg,
Kit van Tulleken, Henry Woodhead
Director of Photography and Research:
John Conrad Weiser

PRESIDENT: Christopher T. Linen
Chief Operating Officer: John M. Fahey Jr.
Senior Vice Presidents: James L. Mercer,
Leopoldo Toralballa
Vice Presidents: Stephen L. Bair, Ralph J. Cuomo,
Terence J. Furlong, Neal Goff, Stephen L. Goldstein,
Juanita T. James, Hallett Johnson III, Robert H.
Smith, Paul R. Stewart
Director of Production Services:
Robert J. Passantino

Library of Congress Cataloguing in Publication Data
When others care for your child.
    (Successful parenting)
    Bibliography: p.
    Includes index.
    1. Working mothers — United States. 2. Child care
services — United States. I. Time-Life Books.
II. Series.
HQ759.48.W48 1987   649'.1   86-30077
ISBN 0-8094-5920-5
ISBN 0-8094-5921-3 (lib. bdg.)

Successful Parenting

SERIES DIRECTOR: Donia Ann Steele
Deputy Editor: Jim Hicks
Series Administrator: Norma E. Shaw
Editorial Staff for *When Others Care for Your Child:*
Designer: Raymond Ripper
Picture Editors: Neil Kagan (principal),
Blaine Marshall
Text Editor: Robert A. Doyle
Researchers: Myrna Traylor-Herndon (principal),
Roxie France-Nuriddin, Karen Monks
Assistant Designer: Susan Gibas
Copy Coordinators: Marfé Ferguson,
Carolee Belkin Walker
Picture Coordinator: Bradley Hower
Editorial Assistant: Jenester C. Lewis

Special Contributors: Laura Akgulian,
Amy Goodwin Aldrich, Charlotte Anker, Wendy
Murphy, Susan Perry, David Thiemann, Enid Yurman
(text); Melva Holloman, Anne Muñoz-Furlong,
Gail Prensky, Marjorie Elizabeth Py (research);
Paul Graboff (design).

Editorial Operations
Copy Chief: Diane Ullius
Editorial Operations Manager: Caroline A. Boubin
Production: Celia Beattie
Library: Louise D. Forstall

Correspondents: Elisabeth Kraemer-Singh (Bonn);
Maria Vincenza Aloisi (Paris); Ann Natanson
(Rome).

First printing. Printed in U.S.A.

Published simultaneously in Canada.
School and library distribution by
Silver Burdett Company, Morristown,
New Jersey 07960.

TIME-LIFE is a trademark of Time
Incorporated U.S.A.

Other Publications

FIX IT YOURSELF
FITNESS, HEALTH & NUTRITION
HEALTHY HOME COOKING
UNDERSTANDING COMPUTERS
LIBRARY OF NATIONS
THE ENCHANTED WORLD
THE KODAK LIBRARY OF CREATIVE PHOTOGRAPHY
GREAT MEALS IN MINUTES
THE CIVIL WAR
PLANET EARTH
COLLECTOR'S LIBRARY OF THE CIVIL WAR
THE EPIC OF FLIGHT
THE GOOD COOK
WORLD WAR II
HOME REPAIR AND IMPROVEMENT
THE OLD WEST

*For information on and a full description
of any of the Time-Life Books series listed
above, please write:*
Reader Information
Time-Life Books
541 North Fairbanks Court
Chicago, Illinois 60611

This volume is one of a series about raising children.

*The emergency first-aid instructions
appearing on pages 132-135 of this book are
not meant to substitute for formal training
in first aid. Professional emergency
assistance should always be summoned in
cases of serious breathing difficulty,
illness or injury.*

The Consultants

General Consultants

Dr. Bettye Caldwell, overall consultant for *When Others Care for Your Child,* is an internationally recognized authority in the field of child care. She established the first U.S. infant day-care center in Syracuse, New York, in 1964, and as President of the National Association for the Education of Young Children, she helped develop the now-standard accreditation process for quality day-care centers. Dr. Caldwell direct- ed a center in a neighborhood public school in Little Rock, Arkansas, that became the model for such facilities throughout the nation, and she has been involved in creating public policy on day-care issues. Current- ly Donaghey Distinguished Professor of Education at the University of Arkansas at Little Rock, she travels throughout Europe, the Middle East and Asia, studying day-care projects in other countries and cultures.

Special Consultants

Dr. Anne Harris Cohn, who gave her expert view on child sexual abuse, is Executive Director of the National Committee for Prevention of Child Abuse. A former White House fellow and special assistant to the Secretary of the Department of Health and Human Services, Dr. Cohn directed the first national evaluation of child-abuse and neglect treat- ment programs and has contributed to public policy on the issue.

Frances Litman, who advised on the section about working parents and contributed her expertise on quality time, directs the Center for Parenting Studies at Wheelock College in Boston. She has written and lectured widely on the problems of two-career families and conducts "Seminars at the Workplace," a corporate education program for em- ployees seeking to balance work and family life.

Dr. Daniel W. Ochsenschlager, Medical Director of Emergency Ser- vices at the Children's Hospital National Medical Center in Washington, D.C., assisted with the material advising baby-sitters about medical con- cerns. He also serves as an associate professor of child health and devel- opment at the George Washington University School of Medicine.

Contributors to the Experts' Discussion of Day Care

Dr. Jay Belsky, Professor of Human Development at Pennsylvania State University, has done considerable research into the effects of day care on the emotional development of infants and the impact of day care on families. Dr. Belsky has testified before Congress regarding his findings.

Dr. T. Berry Brazelton, a pediatrician, is Chief of the Child Develop- ment Unit at The Children's Hospital, Boston, and Clinical Professor of Pediatrics at Harvard Medical School. Dr. Brazelton is the author of several books on parent-child relationships, including *Working and Caring* and *Infants and Mothers.*

Ellen Galinsky is Project Director of the Work and Family Life Study of Bank Street College of Education in New York City. Family stresses and supports are the themes of her recent book, *The New Extended Family: Day Care That Works,* and of much of her research and lecturing.

Dr. Sandra Wood Scarr is Chairman of the Department of Psychology at the University of Virginia in Charlottesville. Editor of the professional journal, *Developmental Psychology,* she is the author of *Mother Care/ Other Care,* a study of child care that won the National Book Award of the American Psychological Association in 1985.

Dr. Burton L. White, Director of the Center for Parent Education in Newton, Massachusetts, is concerned with the effects of child-rearing practices on the development of competence in children. He has pub- lished extensively on early childhood development, and his book, *The First Three Years of Life,* was nominated in 1975 for the Pulitzer Prize.

Dr. Edward F. Zigler is Sterling Professor of Psychology at Yale Univer- sity and Director of the Bush Center in Child Development and Social Policy. His recent articles deal with problems of child abuse and exam- ine infant day care and its effects on parent-child attachment.

Contents

4 Baby-Sitters 92

5 A Baby-Sitter's Guide 106

Perspectives on Child Care

However remote or unlikely the prospect may seem when you first cradle your precious newborn in your arms, a time will come when you will leave your child in someone else's care. It may be for just a few hours on an occasional Saturday night, while you take in a movie; or it might be from morning to evening, five days a week, as you return to the career you had before you became a parent. Whatever the circumstances, you will want to be sure that the caregiver standing in for you is providing the protection and loving attention that your child needs, not dumping a wide-awake baby into his crib to get him out of the way or plopping an older youngster in front of a television set to keep him quiet. This book will help you plan for, find and make the best use of the kind of supplementary child care that you can feel sure about.

Supplementary care comes in many forms, but most of it falls into two broad categories: baby-sitting and day care. Baby-sitters generally look after your children on an irregular basis and for short periods, often while your child is sleeping. Day care, because it involves longer periods on a regular schedule, has the potential for much greater influence on a child's development. Thus day care is of much more intense concern to most parents, and it is the first topic discussed in this volume.

Changing Patterns of Child Care

If you are considering arranging some kind of supplementary day care for your young child so that you can return to work or take up an academic course or some other pursuit, you are far from alone. The traditional, idealized American family, with an aproned mother at home looking after her young children full time, playing games, teaching discipline and kissing away hurts, is a fast-vanishing phenomenon.

In the United States today, more than half the mothers of children younger than six years of age are employed outside the home. In fact, about half the mothers of infants younger than one year old go out to work.

The people who provide day care for these children include a few househusband fathers (some by choice, some because their wives can find work while they cannot) and a scattering of au pair girls or other live-in helpers. Mostly, however, the caregivers are neighbors who operate small, sometimes unlicensed, child-care operations in their homes; relatives of the child who may volunteer to do the job for free; caregivers who are paid to stay at the child's home while the youngster's parents are at work; and day-care centers, which range from nonprofit groups that are run by churches or other community institutions to nationwide commercial chains.

Whatever day-care arrangement or combination of arrangements you select for your youngster, you will want to be certain that it ensures a safe and caring environment, one in which your child will thrive and be happy. You probably already know that some authorities believe the only truly suitable environment for a youngster is in his own home with one of his own parents, at least until he is three or four years old, while other authorities maintain that good nonparental day care not only does not harm but may offer special advantages to the child. Before going on to explore aspects of child development that relate to those issues and hearing what the experts have to say, it may help to step back and view the whole subject from a certain distance.

Putting day care in perspective The practice of having people other than parents care for children is neither new nor restricted to any one culture. Before the dawn of history, groups of hunter-gatherers undoubtedly shared child-minding responsibilities to free some mothers for other chores, just as communities practicing primitive agriculture in undeveloped areas still do.

Many industrialized nations, both Western and Eastern, have long been providing day-care services through highly organized, extensive systems. And the care these systems provide is not necessarily as impersonal as it may appear from a distance. Certainly, highly reputed child-development authorities have found much to admire in the day nurseries of Israel's kibbutzim and Sweden's factories and offices.

In fact, when viewed from a global perspective, the notion that young children should spend their days at home in the exclusive company of their siblings and mother — the American 1950s TV sitcom concept of family — was never very widespread. Mothers, it is true, historically have provided the primary care for their youngsters, but usually in the company of other mothers and their children, or within the supporting framework of an extended family, with aunts, grandmothers and older siblings to care for young children. And throughout history, those families who could afford the expense have also employed wet

Where the Children Spend Their Days

As the graph at right illustrates, since the 1950s the kinds of day care preferred by mothers who work full time have changed dramatically. In that decade, more than half the children too young for school were looked after in their own homes. By the early 1980s, only about a fourth stayed at home. Meanwhile, placing the youngster in another person's home has become the most popular choice, and the use of licensed day-care centers has increased steadily. The reason for the change may be partly the rising cost of paying a caregiver to spend all day at a youngster's home and partly an increased parental awareness that being in a group can stimulate a child's social and intellectual development.

At home

Another home

Group care

100

percent

0

1950   1960   1970   1980

nurses, nannies and other nonfamily members to watch over their children.

The history of American day care

Day-care centers began to appear in the United States in the 19th century, mainly in order to serve the children of mothers working in the new factories of the Industrial Revolution. Many of those women were immigrants who had left their extended families in the Old Country; there were no grandmothers at home to look after the young ones. Most of the early day-care centers offered only custodial care — a modest meal, a change of diapers, someone to keep the children out of harm's way — and there were not many of them. Fewer than 200 centers existed at the turn of the century.

Most of them were run by private charities. The first public funds for day care did not become available until the Great Depression in the 1930s, when day-care centers were established to provide jobs for unemployed teachers, nurses, cooks and janitors. By 1937, some 40,000 children were being cared for in about 1,900 centers across the country. But the first real day-care boom in the United States came with World War II, when women marched into the factories to fill the places of men who went to war. By the end of the war, more than 1.5 million children were in day-care facilities of varying quality, most of which were publicly funded.

But in 1945 when the men came back to their jobs, the majority of the women returned home and most of the day-care centers closed. Working mothers had to scramble to find day care for their children in the homes of neighbors or relatives or the few private centers.

It was not until the mid-1960s that changes in America's political, social and economic climate again began to greatly increase both the number of women employed outside the home and the number of day-care facilities. Enrollment in licensed centers doubled, for example, between 1967 and 1970. And unlike the purely custodial centers of the past, many of the new day-care centers offered activities to promote healthy intellectual, emotional and social development. Child-care operations in homes proliferated even more rapidly.

The situation today

The forces spurring the new growth in supplementary child care that began during the 1960s are even stronger now. More mothers are employed outside the home than ever before. The proportion of mothers in the labor force with children younger than the age of six increased from about 20 percent in 1960

A father delivering his older child to a caregiver confronts guilt-inducing resistance from the youngster. As the number of working mothers increases, more fathers are sharing child-care chores — including having to experience the emotional anguish of scenes like this.

to more than 50 percent in the mid-1980s. Part of the reason is money. Because of inflation and other economic changes, as well as increased expectations, many middle-class couples believe that two incomes are needed to maintain a family standard of living comparable to what one earner could provide in the 1950s. About 12 million American children live in single-parent homes nowadays; the single parent, in most cases a mother, usually has to hold a job to make ends meet.

Money is not the only factor dictating these patterns, however. In one survey, more than half the working mothers questioned said they would continue to work even without the financial incentive. Autonomy, personal growth and a sense of accomplishment were among the reasons cited for wanting to work. Today's parents, especially mothers, have been characterized as less child-oriented than previous generations, not so willing to sacrifice their own career plans or other personal goals for the sake of their children. Many of them convincingly contend, however, that they do not love their children less; they simply believe that happy, self-fulfilled parents are more likely to produce happy, self-assured children.

The factors that have caused more and more mothers to work outside the home have coincided with increased mobility and fragmentation of families. Not only are aunts and grandmothers not likely to reside under the same roof as younger family members, they may live halfway across the continent. And anyway, the working mother's mother, even if she lives just down the block, may very well have a job of her own. It is little wonder that the demand for day care keeps growing. ⁘

How Day Care Affects a Child

Before handing over her baby, a mother eyes the caregiver with a mix of trust and unease. Some misgivings are natural at the start of such a relationship, even though the parent has already met the caregiver and thoroughly checked her references.

What effects, if any, does day care have on young children? In the whole subject of child development, no other topic simmers with so much contentious emotion. One reason is that the question is personal: Few parents want to hear that whatever decisions they make about day care may not be the most beneficial for their children. It is also political, being deeply entangled with such issues as women's equality, preservation of the family as an institution, welfare programs and taxes. Even child-development researchers sometimes seem to overstep the bounds of scientific objectivity in their commitment to one point of view or another.

In fact, the question as stated above may never be conclusively answered, because it is far too simplistic. Day care is not a single, uniform experience that is the same for all children. It comes in many different forms — in as many forms, it could be argued, as there are people or establishments providing it. And the effect that any supplementary caregiver has on a given child is also inextricably bound up with the child's own personality, parents and home environment. Still, child-development researchers make diligent attempts to identify and to measure the effects of day care as best they can.

The importance of attachment

Many studies focus on whether day care affects a child's attachment to her mother, and if so, how. Attachment is the result of the bonding process between an infant and her most important caregivers, usually her parents and in particular her mother. Attachment creates an emotional haven from which the child can confidently explore her world, knowing that if anything frightens or distresses her, she can retreat to be picked up and reassured. It has been shown that babies develop strong attachments by eight to 10 months of age. The strength of the attachment to the mother or other primary caregiver is thought to be an important clue to how the child will fare later in social and intellectual development. Studies indicate that a securely attached child is likely to have more confidence in her abilities and in her capacity to form relationships with others, while children with insecure attachments may be more easily frustrated by challenges and less cooperative with their parents.

To measure attachment, researchers frequently use a procedure they call the "strange situation," in which a child under laboratory observation experiences brief separations from her mother, encounters with a stranger and reunions with her mother. These and similar experiments involving supplementary caregivers have shown that children can establish loving,

healthy bonds with their daytime caregivers while still reserving their strongest emotional attachment for their own mothers. In such a situation, most children display distress when their mothers leave the room. In similar settings, if both the mother and a favorite caregiver are present, they are more likely to turn to their mother for comfort and consolation.

In at least one aspect of behavior, however, researchers have reported a potentially significant difference between day-care children and children looked after at home by their mothers. When reuniting with their mothers after a separation, day-care toddlers were more likely to avoid immediate affectionate contact. They instead kept their distance and averted their eyes for a while. This behavior was especially prevalent among children who entered day care before they were a year old.

Insecurity — or independence? Some authorities think this avoidance behavior may be a sign that a child is insecurely attached to his mother. If so, they say, then day-care children — particularly if they start day care as infants — may be more likely than other youngsters to develop the problems that insecure attachment can lead to. Authorities can point to other long-term studies. These studies indicate that children who are in day care as infants tend to be more aggressive later with adults and other children, less willing to comply with their mother's wishes, less enthusiastic in taking on challenges and less persistent in trying to solve difficult problems.

But other child-development experts take a completely different view of some of the same evidence. They say that any tendency on the part of a day-care child to avoid his mother after a brief separation may not signal an insecure attachment at all. It may instead mean that the child is simply used to separations and reunions from daily experience and that he is exhibiting an impressively mature sense of independence. And to bolster their viewpoint, they can cite studies that show day-care children tend to be more at ease and less timid when encountering youngsters they have not met before and more self-assured in the presence of adults. There is even some research that suggests children in day care get a jump on the stay-at-homes in intellectual development, although it is a short-lived advantage that is eroded within a few years.

A round-up of experts' opinions appears on pages 16-19. While you ponder all the conflicting points of view and wonder what they may or may not mean to your own children, consider also this: Child-development authorities are among the first to point out that any or maybe even all of the studies that lead to those varying opinions could be challenged for lack of scientific validity, since the field research is necessarily so imprecise and subject to so many uncontrollable variables.

Some known factors   Although the experts — and many parents — differ on whether the effects of day care, on balance, are generally positive or negative, some aspects of the question are not disputed, or at least not so widely disputed. Take the effect on health, for instance: There is no doubt that a child in any kind of group care is going to be exposed to a lot more contagious ailments than one who stays at home. Parents and caregivers need to take special precautions to counter this problem *(page 60)*.

There is also substantial agreement that the age at which a child begins day care and the proportion of her time that is spent away from her parents are important in figuring how the experience will affect her. Few authorities feel that a child two and a half or three years old will suffer any significant ill effects from spending several half-days a week in some kind of organized play group. In fact, most children of that age need the companionship and stimulation of their peers in order to maintain a normal pace of emotional and social development; if they are not in an organized group, they should at least have a busy social schedule that includes frequent visits to the homes of other children.

Between three and six years, adjusting to day care becomes easier still as children develop better language skills and acquire a concept of time. When you tell your four-year-old that you will pick her up from nursery school after naptime, she will have a fair idea of how long you will be gone. Still, a new environment can be stressful, even for a well-adjusted five-year-old, and may lead to anxiety — and a few tears — when a parent departs.

Timing day care for babies   While experts disagree about the long-term effects of day care on infants and young toddlers, some periods of early life do seem better than others for starting it. An infant begins to recognize familiar faces sometime between three and five months of age. Her preferences for specific people, however, do not attain full strength for another three months or so. When this happens, attachments are obvious. The baby of eight to 10 months loves to be cuddled by her parents — in most cases, especially by her mother — and by other very familiar people to whom she has become attached. But she may protest wildly when less familiar people get too close, even relatives who a few months earlier were able to elicit smiles every time they picked her up.

No one should take offense. Her objections are a sign that she has achieved attachment, an important developmental milestone. But her attitude does make it difficult to introduce a new caregiver into her life. It also means her parents may have to put up with howls of distress any time they leave her, because along with attachment comes what is known as separation anxiety. Mentally and emotionally, the baby has developed enough to recognize and love a familiar face, but not enough to understand that when the familiar face disappears, it is not gone forever. That understanding usually comes between 15 and 24 months, and it is then that separation anxiety will begin to wane.

So the period from about eight months to around 15 to 18 months may be a particularly difficult time for a child to start day care. If you plan to place your child part of the time in someone else's care during this period, be prepared for some vigorous protest. And if you are not put off by the concerns of some authorities about children entering day care during the first year, you may want to initiate supplementary care well before your baby demonstrates strong attachment and separation anxiety. Around six months is thought to be a favorable time for most children. By then they should have developed a solid foundation for their attachment to their mothers but probably are not yet spooked by new faces in their lives. Even if you are not planning to return to work until your baby is, say, a year old, you may be able to ease the transition for her by introducing the caregiver on at least a part-time basis at around six months.

Several factors besides age affect whether a child will have difficulty accepting nonparental care. Some children, just by disposition, have trouble in new situations. One mother, whose eldest son went skipping happily off to nursery school at the age of three, found that her second son threw tantrums when placed in the same school at the same age. The sex of a child is also important: Boys seem to have more trouble than girls separating from their parents.

One of the most important influences on how a child reacts to supplementary care is the nature and quality of the care itself. A child entering a loving environment full of warmth, fun and stimulation is more likely to benefit and less likely to fuss than a child whose emotional and intellectual needs are not met by the care arrangements. Another important factor is the attitude of the child's parents — not only whether they have confidence in the specific caregiver, but whether they are confident that their decision to turn to day care at all was the best thing to do for their child, given the family's circumstances. ∴

An Expert's View

The Debate over Day Care

Whether one parent should stay home with the children or both should feel free to work outside the home is a question that provokes strong emotions. Child-development specialists are as divided on the issue as parents who are faced with the decision. Following is a sampling of some authoritative voices who have weighed in on the debate.

A Multitude of Factors at Work

In our culture, we tend to think about the effects of day care in black and white: Some experts say it's harmful, others say it's great. I believe it is somewhere in the middle. The effects depend on the specific circumstances of the child care, the family life and the parents' jobs.

It is extraordinarily difficult to draw clear-cut conclusions from the current research on the effects of day care. The reason for this is that a child's responses to care outside the home are affected by many other factors. One of the pivotal factors is your attitude toward using day care in the first place. If you think that it is terrible and feel unusual anxiety about being away from the home, those emotions can affect your child. Another factor is job stress. Such things as job insecurity, the relationship you have with your supervisor, the demands of your job and the amount of control you have over your work can make a big difference in your mental and physical health. That, in turn, can affect your child. The other stresses in your life — money worries, moving, marital discord and so forth — can have an impact as well. In short, many of the effects that research tends to attribute to child care are just as likely to be caused by other factors.

At its best, day care is not substitute care, it is supplemental care. The best day-care providers understand that it is the parents who are rearing the child, and they see themselves as a support system. In this framework the day-care provider becomes, in a real sense, a part of the child's extended family. That is the kind of support that good day care really provides, and if you find this sort of help, you have a big advantage.

Ellen Galinsky, M.S.
Director, Work and Family Studies
Bank Street College of Education, New York

Stay at Home for at Least Four Months

There are critical stages in the development of mothering, just as there are important stages in a baby's development. In order to feel competent as a parent and truly attached to her child, a mother needs to go through this learning process before returning to work. The same probably holds true for fathers — though I have not studied that question fully.

When a mother is able to devote full attention to nurturing her child through the first months of life, the baby learns to trust his environment, the mother learns to trust herself as a caregiver, and the two of them are likely to become profoundly attached to one another. Although we have little research data to confirm it, we believe that once the initial trust and attachment are established, the mother may be ready to share the baby's care with other people. The infant may also be ready to profit from time spent in the care of others. But the attachment process cannot be shortchanged without posing serious risks to the development of both child and mother.

The first three months with a new child are generally an exhausting time for the parents. They are just getting to know their baby and are not yet adept at anticipating his moods and needs. They have not had time to grow accustomed to the baby's patterns — the predictable times when he will be cranky, hungry or tired. I feel that it is important for the primary caregiver to be at home through this difficult period, gradually acquiring an intimate familiarity with the baby's style and personality.

The fourth month is also crucial. At this point the baby is a little more settled and spends more time in playful interaction. Now the mother gets repeated opportunities to see that the baby's smiles and vocalizations are meant especially for her. If a substitute caregiver helps the baby through the hard times of settling in and then shares the child's first playful moments as well, it is not likely that the mother will feel fully in control of her demanding new role as parent.

In general, the longer a mother can stay home with her baby, the more she will feel that the baby is "hers" and the more intimacy she will share with him. I could wish for some time for fathers to be at home, too, to establish a similar kind of interdependency. Obviously, economic and practical considerations also affect the decision to go back to work. Parents who provide an adequate living for their children feel more secure in the role of caregiver, and such feelings of security are also crucial to the attachment process. Research shows, too, that the working woman who carries home a sense of competence and satisfaction from her job is able to feel like a more complete person and thus is able to be a more nurturing mother. The decision to return to work therefore must take into account the demands and opportunities of the parent's work environment.

T. Berry Brazelton, M.D.
Director, Child Development Unit
The Children's Hospital, Boston

Only Parents or Grandparents Will Do

In most instances, day care simply is not in the best interest of children under 30 months of age. It was created, after all, to meet newly perceived needs of parents — not because we were looking for a better way to raise our children. Care outside the home will always be necessary in extremely difficult family circumstances — with alcoholic or abusive parents, for example. Wherever there is an option, however, I feel that it should be used very sparingly, if at all, in the first six months of a child's life. Beyond six months of age, substitute care should be limited to no more than three to four hours a day, five days a week, for the balance of the first two-and-a-half years.

At stake during these early months is the development of the capacity to love another person. And what a child needs most to achieve this development is ready access to somebody who is absolutely crazy about her. Parents and grandparents are the only ones who really fit the bill.

When it comes to infants, good day care can only be delivered by carefully selected, well-trained, highly talented and reasonably well-paid personnel. Certainly, no more than two infants should be entrusted to any single caregiver at a time. Unfortunately, it is not likely that you are going to find much of this sort of high-quality care available. If you do, it will probably be very expensive. The usual solution, of course, is to assign more infants to each caregiver and thus lower

the cost. But if a substitute caregiver has two, three or more infants to care for, and one of them is ill or out of sorts, it becomes virtually impossible to provide prompt attention to the needs of the other children.

Burton L. White, Ph.D.
Director, Center for Parent Education
Newton, Massachusetts

Children Thrive in Good Day Care

Whether by choice or necessity, the majority of mothers with preschool children now work outside the home. Happily, it is possible for these parents to find good care for their children. Locating suitable day care often demands a fair amount of shopping around and a willingness to stay well informed about the changing needs of your children. Babies do thrive in good day care, just as they do at home with an attentive mother. Secure attachments to others in addition to the parents provides emotional backup at times when a mother is not immediately available.

I see children as sturdy individuals whose development is shaped by a complex interplay of biology and experience. They can do well in a wide variety of caregiving situations. Parents play a crucial role in the development of their children, but it is not an exclusive role. In most other cultures — and sometimes in our own — there is not the same stress on a mother's exclusive ability to guarantee normal development. We have blown this idea out of proportion.

Good child care is just that — good care. Who administers the care and where it takes place are not nearly so important as the quality. The care that you give your child may enhance her development to some extent, but it cannot radically reshape her inborn potential. With good care she will grow up to be herself — her own unique combination of heredity and experiences. It is folly to try to take either total credit or full blame for all that your child becomes. You do not have that much control over her development. Worrying about leaving your child while you go to work, even in very good care, is understandable given the current preconceptions of our culture. But it is worry misspent.

Sandra Scarr, Ph.D.
Chairman, Department of Psychology
University of Virginia

What Kind of Care Can You Really Find?

Is day care good or bad for infants and toddlers? Parents and policy makers would like experts to answer this question with a straight yes or no, but the answers vary with the age of the child in question and the quality of care. In any case, based on research to date, experts can give no simple answer. Research has consistently shown that good day care is less likely to be harmful and that bad day care is certain to be. We have to realize that parents of young children work out of economic necessity and rely on their incomes to support their children. In the face of these facts, there is consensus among child-development experts that in a stable family situation, it is optimal for parents to care for their young infants for the first three or four months of life. Many families today are unable to survive economically on one income, however. If we are to ensure familial stability, we must make early care for children financially feasible.

When older infants and toddlers enter day care, only a small percentage attend the high-quality, university-based centers where the majority of research is conducted. Most are in informal baby-sitting arrangements or family day-care homes, which are largely unlicensed, unmonitored and out of the view of researchers. The quality in such homes can probably be best characterized as heterogeneous, with most care falling in the midrange of mediocrity. As it stands now, parents bear most of the burden of finding and evaluating child care. Parents cannot effectively do this alone. Families are the heart of our social order, and as a society, we must ensure that the best quality care is accessible to children from all segments of society.

Edward F. Zigler, Ph.D.
Director, Bush Center in Child Development and Social Policy
Yale University

There is Ample Room for Concern

In my opinion, we have to be extremely cautious in drawing conclusions from research on the effects that day care has on children. Any of the effects that can be attributed to a youngster's being cared for outside the home can also be associated with a host of other factors in the child's life. Furthermore, I believe that it is important to recognize that few individuals — researchers included — are truly open-minded when it comes to the subject of infant day care. The topic is simply too emotionally charged for all involved.

Such cautions notwithstanding, I am becoming increasingly concerned by the steady flow of disconcerting new evidence. When I reviewed the research literature in 1977 and again in 1980, I found little cause for concern. This is no longer the case. There is a pattern to the findings of recent studies in that child care, especially when it is begun in the first year, is often associated with a tendency of infants to avoid or maintain a distance from their mothers. Admittedly, scientists differ in their interpretations of this discovery: Some view the behavior as evidence of early maturity, demonstrating an ability to adapt to the day-care environment. Others interpret the avoidance behavior much more negatively, suggesting that nonmaternal care in the first year may jeopardize the quality of the mother-child bond and thereby endanger a child's future development.

I feel that the research is not yet sufficient for us to know with certainty which interpretation is correct. However, I do think that there is ample room for concern. I feel that an empirical case can be made that early infant care may cause insecurity in the attachment relationship and that it may also be associated with diminished compliance and cooperation with adults, increased aggressiveness and possibly even greater social maladjustment in the preschool and early school years. These are by no means inevitable outcomes: Many children who are in day care do not show such effects. Unfortunately, we do not yet know exactly under which conditions these problems are most likely to occur. Presumably, the quality and stability of the care make a difference.

Jay Belsky, Ph.D.
Professor of Human Development
Pennsylvania State University

Weighing the Decision to Return to Work

When you are deciding whether to return to work and share the care of your child with someone else, you must consider other factors besides the effect that day care may have on your youngster. You also have to take into account how the decision will affect you and your family, because those effects ultimately will be felt by your child, in some form or other.

It is reassuring to remember that you can change your mind if your first plan does not work out — if circumstances permit, of course. A mother who thought she could take her newborn to the office for the first three months, when he would be sleeping much of the time, quickly discovers that his demands interfere drastically with her work. She begins to look for infant day care. Another mother, who carefully made arrangements to return to work after six months, finds herself, when the day of separation finally arrives, unwilling to leave her baby in someone else's care. She cancels her child's slot in a local day-care center. Your attitude about parenting and outside employment can change markedly; whatever your original decision, do not be reluctant to reassess it occasionally.

It is best not to make such an important decision right after giving birth. Hormonal changes, lack of sleep and numerous other stresses that come with a newborn child can make it difficult for you to weigh your options and find your true feelings about balancing parenthood and career.

Do you have a choice? Many women who go back to work after the birth of a baby have no other choice; family finances compel them to start earning again. This is particularly true in single-parent families, but many other, two-parent households also depend on the woman's income to make ends meet. If financial need is your only reason for leaving your child in someone else's care, however, first make a thorough examination of your family budget. You may find that some of the necessities do not seem quite so necessary when measured against the rewards you expect to derive from caring for your child yourself. Some families making such a reassessment decide they can get along with one car instead of two or even move to a less expensive neighborhood so that a parent can stay home to look after the child.

Make sure you know how much supplementary care is going to cost if you do return to work. Good child care can be expensive. Some couples find it costs so much that they simply cannot afford to have both parents working unless both are high earners, especially when other expenses such as transportation and maintaining a work wardrobe are taken into account.

Some clear-cut attitudes

Maybe you already are sure what you want to do. Some women, perhaps because of their own upbringing, their personalities or what they have learned about child rearing, are determined to be full-time caregivers for their children. They feel that raising children is the most important and rewarding job they can undertake, at least until their youngsters are in school.

Others who do not embrace such a traditional viewpoint might realize nonetheless that they would rather stay home and care for their children than return to work. Perhaps their old jobs are not satisfying enough to lure them back. Or they may feel confident that they will not have difficulty finding a good job later, when their children are older, and decide to try this full-time mothering experience while they have a chance.

Other women, who love their children just as much, may know with equal conviction that they definitely want to return to work. If you are one of them, you may feel comfortable about sharing the care of your children with others, as long as the supplementary care is of high quality. It is likely that you have a job you enjoy, and perhaps you feel you cannot afford to lose momentum in your career. Or you may just thrive on the excitement of your work and find the prospect of staying home, even in the company of your wonderful new child, somewhat stifling.

Weighing the decision

Even if you are convinced from the beginning about staying home or returning to work, take time to consider the possible results of your choice. And make sure you explore the question with your spouse. Although in most families it is the mother who bears the brunt of the decision, by giving up her career or by working a full day while still trying to be her child's primary caregiver, both parents must be committed to the arrangement in order to make it work.

Fathers, too, have convictions about what is best for the child and the family. Some may dread the thought of trying to keep the household operating on one income when two have been necessary up until now and will want their wives to return to work. Others have strong, traditional opinions about a mother's role. One woman who longed to go back to her career lamented: "The problem is my husband, who wants his child to have a 'real mother.' " A woman who is going to carry the greatest burden of the consequences can rightly insist on having the biggest say in the decision, but both parents must somehow come to an agreement. If a mother chooses to return to work in spite of her husband's objections, perhaps he may opt to become a househusband and look after the child himself.

Guilt and regrets

Whatever choice a mother makes, she should be prepared to experience some doubt and second thoughts. Women who stay at home with their children often resentfully feel that their contribution is disparaged by society. They sometimes wonder if they were right to choose *Sesame Street* over Wall Street and frequently find themselves being defensive, especially when they meet women with professional jobs. Some may also feel guilty because they are not bringing money into the family — although this feeling usually crops up only when a mother is spending her husband's earnings to buy something for herself.

Working mothers may worry that their youngsters are not getting enough love and attention and that somehow the children will be emotionally or intellectually stunted as a result. Or they regret not being present for some of the developmental milestones in their children's lives: the first smile, the first step or the look of delight on a child's face when he first recognizes the letters of his own name.

There is really not much you can do about the doubt and guilt except to expect them and remember that you would probably experience them whichever course you decided to follow. You should also anticipate some other likely problems and advantages of each alternative.

The working mother: pluses and minuses

The primary rewards of going out to work are fairly apparent. The family probably will have more net income. And the mother who likes her job will enjoy a sense of fulfillment. Some advantages are not so immediately obvious. Studies have shown, for instance, that daughters benefit from having a working mother as a role model. They develop more confidence, tend to get better grades and later are more inclined to pursue careers of their own than are daughters of nonworking mothers.

Whether being a working mother is more of a plus or a minus depends very much on your job. Does it allow you to choose your own hours within certain limits, to work occasionally at home or to take off a day or so when your child is sick? If not, and if your spouse's job is also inflexible, one of you may want to look into other job possibilities. Do not try to change immediately, though. It is difficult enough to adjust to a new baby without having to adjust to a new job at the same time.

While flexibility in your job is helpful, if you are truly interested in a career you must beware of putting obstacles in your own path. Some working mothers find themselves turning down promotions that require more responsibility. Some of them confess they do so because they feel that accepting more responsibility

Parent to Parent

Going Back to the Office

❝ It was heart wrenching returning to work. I'd look at photos of my baby and moon over them. But I've thought about what it would be like to stay home all the time and it frightens me. You get boxed into your house, and that becomes your world. ❞

❝ I went back to work six weeks after my first child and four weeks after my second, but a few months later I quit my job. I found it difficult to constantly shift gears from career woman to mother, because you have to change your evaluation of accomplishment. When you're a mother, there may be no tangible accomplishment in a day or week, and still you've done something important for your children. Two years and one more child later, I'm still very happy. ❞

❝ My baby was 10 months old when I went back to work. I wish I had been home in that wonderful second year when they do all those things — walking and talking and everything all at once. I missed all that. When it starts happening, it's like popcorn popping. It just explodes, and I wish I hadn't missed it. ❞

❝ I loved spending time with my wonderful new daughter, but after six months at home, I was beginning to feel like my husband's secretary. I missed my exciting job and being financially independent. So even though we didn't need the money, we agreed that I would go back to work and that we would get an au pair and she would be our housewife. Although not a perfect solution, it relieved my mind so I could go back to work. ❞

❝ I'm a consultant and I work about three days a week. It's an ideal situation. I work for my sanity. As much as I love my children, it helps me to be with my peers. My children still get plenty of me. My life revolves around them. ❞

❝ I have an MBA and have held several management jobs with large corporations, and I couldn't conceive of staying at home. I kept telling myself that the quality of life for our family depended on my working. But once I had the baby, I realized that the quality of our lives depended on my being at home. I love challenges and it's certainly a challenge to stay home. You have to educate yourself to do it; we aren't trained for it and it really isn't easy. ❞

❝ My wife and I realized that her employee benefits were greater than mine and my potential for freelance work was better than hers, and so we decided I would stay home. Now, two years later, I have mixed emotions. I'm very happy to see so much of my son, but my career is suffering and I feel embarrassed because I'm not out there making money. I also have come to believe that children belong with their mothers. When my wife comes home, my son clings to her. There is something the child has with his mother and not his father or anybody else. ❞

in the workplace would mean stealing more of themselves from their children.

However, if your reason for sharing your child's care with someone else is to advance your career, then you get the worst of both worlds if you let guilt stop your progress. One way to combat this tendency is to work out a career-progress timetable, setting job goals keyed to the development and growing independence of your child.

Advantages and disadvantages of staying home

The big plus in not returning to work is that you become your child's full-time caregiver, which offers emotional bonuses for both of you. Not only are you present for all those memorable learning experiences, but you know the quality of care your youngster is receiving. You are not tortured, as many working mothers are, by fears that the daytime caregiver is ignoring your child's needs. And your child receives the benefit of consistency and continuity; few working mothers can count on their children having the same supplementary caregiver year after year — or in some cases, even month after month.

The biggest disadvantages are measured in money and career advancement. A woman who drops out of the job market for a few years misses not only promotions, but the pay raises that come with those upward moves. Giving up a job to raise children also leaves a woman economically vulnerable if she should become divorced or widowed. She may suddenly find herself forced to take low-paying and emotionally unrewarding work to support her family.

If you and your spouse are used to two incomes, family finances may become an issue between you. A husband, even one who a few months earlier insisted that his wife stay home to care for his child, may wonder aloud just what the family is spending his hard-earned money on. The friction can be compounded by a wife's resentment that her husband goes off to an exciting job among interesting people — namely adults — every day, while she is confined to the seemingly unintellectual and often tedious world of children. One way to reduce the problems caused by these feelings is to discuss them thoroughly with your spouse before making the decision to stay home or to return to work and to continue talking about these issues after a decision has been made. By anticipating the problems that could arise, you can defuse them, or at least minimize their impact.

A mother also needs to look out for any signs that she is directing toward her child the resentment she feels about giving up a career. Some resentment is natural, but it is important not to manifest it in front of the child.

Timing a return to work
Parents who decide to place their child in day care are also faced with the question of when. An employer's parental-leave policy may determine the date; but parents who have leeway should consider a number of factors. One is the anxiety a child may experience with a new caregiver, which seems to be greatest between about eight and 18 months. If you cannot wait until your child is 18 months old or so, it may be advisable to introduce her to supplementary care at about six months, before she develops a fear of new faces.

Also around six months are opportunities to wean an infant

from breast to bottle. During the fifth month, a baby's expanding interest in her environment diverts her attention from the breast, and in the seventh month, a sudden surge in motor development often has the same effect. (You do not necessarily have to give up breast-feeding in order to return to work, however. Many women manage by expressing milk into bottles for feedings or by arranging child care very close to their workplace.)

At about this time, too, a baby's increasing motor control makes her more robust and independent. She may begin to creep or crawl. Her gestures become easier to understand, and her parents gain confidence that someone else is able to take care of her. At the same time, the mother probably will be fully recovered from pregnancy and delivery, and she may be eager to expand her activities to a wider world, even if the child remains the center of it. ❖

Day Care

When you leave your child in someone else's care for three or four or five days a week, you want that care to be the best. You want the assurance that your youngster is physically safe and comfortable in pleasant surroundings and that he is happy and intellectually stimulated — that while you are getting on with your work, your child is getting on with his own growing, learning and playing. The kind of care you want is available. It will take some searching, however, in order to find the best situation for your child and you.

This section of the book is a comprehensive guide designed to help you in your search. It describes the various types of day care available — in-home care, family care and day-care centers — and explains the pros and cons of each. It tells how to find care, how to evaluate what you find, how to help your youngster adjust to it and how to make sure things proceed as smoothly as possible once your child has settled into the situation.

The path, of course, will not always be smooth: No day-care arrangement is perfect all of the time. But if you keep yourself well informed and attentive, and if you are willing to be flexible, you will go a long way toward assuring your child the healthiest possible day care.

A Look at the Options

In-home day care Most parents have an image of the ideal caregiver: A kind, efficient, intelligent woman who lives in their home — or comes to it every day — and devotes her attention to their child while they are at work. They want a modern Mary Poppins. Such in-home caregivers do exist, although it takes searching to find them and, usually, quite a lot of money to keep them.

Some lucky families have an aunt or a grandmother who will do the job and may not even expect a salary. These women usually have not had special training in child development or child care, but often they have raised children of their own and, being volunteers, they are especially loving to the little ones they care for.

For other parents, hiring help is the answer. Some employ au pairs — usually young women, frequently from foreign countries, who care for children in exchange for a small salary and room and board. The au pair's job lies somewhere between that of a relative and that of a servant: She lives on a par (which is what the title means in French) with the family she works for. The American counterparts of au pairs are called mother's helpers. They are often high-school or college students — mostly girls — who usually work full time only during school vacations. Some parents hire housekeeper-caregivers, who do cooking and cleaning as well as child tending.

These people may have had extensive experience with children, but they rarely are professionally trained. The professional in in-home caregiver is a nanny — the Mary Poppins of today. She will have had schooling in child growth and development, in nutrition, and health care and safety, and she will be experienced as well. Nannies rarely do housework, except perhaps the laundry of their charges.

Pros and cons No one would deny that there are wonderful benefits to in-home care. Just the fact that the caregiver comes to you means that you are spared the tiring trips taking your children to and from day care. Your youngster will be exposed to fewer illnesses at home than he would if he spent his day with other children. And the youngster will be in secure, familiar surroundings with a person whose attention and affection are concentrated on him alone.

There are other advantages. In-home caregivers often can be flexible about their hours. If they do

Astride his au pair's shoulders, this youngster rides secure. Au pairs, nannies and other caregivers who come to your home offer children the benefits of undivided attention in addition to familiar surroundings.

not live with you, they may be able to come early and stay late when you must put in extra time at work. Unlike other caregivers, they can be with your child when he is sick, so that you can stay at the office. And those who do housework, of course, relieve you of yet another burden.

But no child-care system is perfect. No matter how kind and attentive your nanny or housekeeper, she cannot provide the same stimulation that the company of a variety of other people — especially other children — gives. Isolation at home is not a problem for infants: A baby thrives on one-to-one attention and needs only occasional outings. Toddlers and older children, however, require bigger challenges; once your child is walking, he will delight in spending part of his time in a play group or in some other organized activity.

This is particularly important if your caregiver is not fluent in English. That can cause practical problems if you do not speak her language, but it also can create difficulties for your child. Although he has an exciting chance to become bilingual, learning a foreign language can slow his development in his own: He will need other English speakers around when he begins to talk.

These and other difficulties, such as finding replacements for caregivers who leave or who become ill, are less important to most people than the fact of expense. Unless your caregiver is a relative, you will find in-home care extremely costly — at least

Your Responsibilities as an Employer

When you hire an in-home caregiver, you have these legal obligations:

- *Wages and hours.* You must pay your in-home caregiver no less than the federal or state minimum wage, whichever is highest. Caregivers must also be paid extra per hour, at least time and a half, if they work more than eight hours per day, or more then 44 hours per week for live-in help. Call your state department of labor in order to obtain more information.

- *Social Security.* If you pay someone more than $50 within a three-month period, you must pay Social Security taxes (FICA) on those wages. Payments must be made every calendar quarter. Both you and your employee are expected to pay equally to the Social Security tax. Be aware, however, that if your employee does not pay her half, the government will later hold you responsible — and charge you

penalties — for the entire amount. For this reason, many parents choose to pay the entire amount for their caregivers, or to withhold the employee's share. You may wish to include these tax payments in figuring out your child-care tax credit *(page 35).* Call your local Social Security office for more information.

- *Unemployment tax.* If you pay someone more than $1,000 within a three-month period, you must pay federal unemployment tax (FUTA). Call the IRS for the proper forms. Some states require employers to pay a state unemployment tax as well. Call your state employment commission for more information.

- *Income tax withholding.* You are not required to withhold federal income taxes from the paychecks of caregivers or other domestic employees. However, you will have to provide a W-2

form (Wage and Tax Statement) to your employee by January 31 and file a copy of this form with the Social Security Administration.

- *Sick leave, vacations and holidays.* Full-time employees must receive a minimum of six days' paid sick leave and six legal holidays each year. Live-in help is entitled to eight holidays per year. After one year of service, your caregiver is also entitled to two weeks' paid vacation.

- *Visas.* Under immigration law, an individual from another country cannot work for you unless that person has a permanent immigrant visa, known as a green card. Sponsoring someone for a green card is a long and difficult process requiring the services of an attorney. Call your local department of labor or the Immigration and Naturalization Service in Washington, D.C., for information.

29

twice as expensive as any other kind of child care. And in addition to salary, you may have to pay worker's compensation insurance in case of injury while on the job. Both you and your employee are required to pay federal taxes, including Social Security taxes.

Finally, if your caregiver is from a foreign country, you must be sure that she has the proper documentation for working in the United States. If you do not meet the various requirements of being an employer, you will be liable to fines and penalties *(box, page 29)*.

Family day care Family day care is just that: It is a system in which women or couples or, more rarely, men take care of children in their homes, often along with their own children. This arrangement has some of the characteristics of a family situation, which is one reason why many experts advocate and many parents choose this type of care. In fact, it is the most widely used type of child care in the United States.

In most states, the quality of the care is to some extent regulated by law. Providers must be licensed and must adhere to rules concerning zoning, safety and sanitation. Usually no more than six children — including the caregivers' own preschool-age children — may be watched by a single person. Sometimes the caregivers operate independently, making their own arrangements about licensing and dealing with parents. In other cases, they are part of a family care system, which is a network of family day-care homes controlled by a private or public agency. The agency trains the caregivers, refers families to them, and generally helps them start and operate their day-care businesses. In these situations, the caregivers are usually paid their salaries by the agency, rather than directly by the parents.

Pros and cons The best family day care will provide a home away from home for your child — a warm, informal, comfortable place where everyday life goes on just as it does in your own house. Here the parent in charge intersperses laundry, dishwashing and other chores with bandaging scraped elbows, serving milk and organizing fingerpainting projects. And your child might have the benefits of playmates around her own age, which she will need as her social skills develop. A good caregiver will do more than just baby-sit. She will provide toys, projects and excursions that help children grow. And as your relationship with her evolves, you will find her a valuable source in understanding your child's moods and development.

Last is the financial aspect of family day care. It is generally the least expensive of all kinds of child care.

There can be drawbacks: Most family day-care homes are unlicensed and thus operate without any supervision. Many parents are unaware of this and do not realize that they need to check for evidence of the day-care home's registration, just as they would check for a license in a child-care center.

Family day-care providers — even licensed ones — must be chosen with the greatest attention to quality. Few have formal training for the job, and although most are parents, they are not necessarily good ones. And there is rarely enough outside supervision of the homes to guarantee that they meet your standards. In some homes, for instance, children receive little intellectual stimulation: They are simply plopped in front of a television set. Some caregivers take in more children than the legal limit — or more than their homes or energies can handle. With family care, you must be the supervisor, and you must be especially alert to the level of the care.

Backup care can be a problem, too. You will usually have to provide it yourself on days when your caregiver is sick or on vacation, unless she has an arrangement with others to stand in for her when she must be off the job.

Day-care centers   Day-care centers are places where children — usually divided according to age — are cared for in groups by people trained in childhood development and early education. Many centers

Relaxed lunches such as this one, in a homey setting with several children, are typical of good family day care. This kind of day care — in which children are tended to in the caregiver's home — is the most popular in the United States today.

combine nursery school with day care, offering an educational program in the morning followed by more loosely structured play activities in the afternoon. Several types of centers can be found. A public center is subsidized and supervised by federal, state or city government. Admission is usually limited to children of low-income families, whose parents pay either no fees or fees based on a sliding scale tied to their income. (Some public school systems also offer extended day school for kindergarteners, in which, for a nominal fee, the children are cared for before and after the school day, on the school grounds.)

Private day-care centers are of two major types: nonprofit and for-profit. Nonprofit centers are usually sponsored by unions, religious organizations, hospitals, universities and the like. For admission, preference is often given to families affiliated with these organizations; there are fees, but they frequently are based on a sliding scale. In recent years, many companies have gone into the business of child care, operating private centers for profit. Some of these are owned by individuals, often husband-and-wife teams. Others are large franchises. These are businesses and their fees are higher than those of other centers; most of the children come from middle- or upper-income families, although some centers have government subsidies so that they can admit children of families who cannot pay their prices.

There are also centers run by parent cooperatives. They are controlled by parents who provide operating funds, hire staff and put in time themselves working with the children or maintaining the facility. Fees at these centers are set by the participating parents. For the most part, such cooperative day-care centers are run by families who do not need all-day, every-day care for their children.

Centers provide more structure than other kinds of day care. They are licensed and supervised, their staffs are trained and their activities planned. Even the number of children is regulated. At most centers, group sizes are no larger than 12 for infants and toddlers, 14 for two- and three-year-olds, 20 for four- and five-year-olds and 24 for six-year-olds. But even structured as they are, the good centers still view themselves as an extension of the family and give each child enough freedom to develop at her own pace.

Pros and cons A good day-care center can have wonderful benefits for a child *(pages 46-49)*. The setting is designed to help a child learn and grow, and as children interact with others of similar ages, they enjoy a rich variety of age-appropriate activities that help pre-

A good day-care center gives children a range of structured activities as well as security and warmth and an opportunity for free play. You should look for a center with a well-trained, stable staff who can help your youngster grow and develop.

pare them for school. The licensing requirements specify that centers must offer educational programs.

There are benefits for parents, too. Centers are reliable. They open and close at set hours each working day and sometimes on holidays. And you will not have to worry about backup care. If a caregiver leaves or falls ill, the center will provide a substitute.

Still, there are drawbacks. When your child spends each day with many other children, he will be exposed to more illnesses and will bring home more sniffles and colds, cases of chicken pox and other childhood ailments. Many centers have a high turnover of staff because day-care employees are underpaid. The lack of consistency this causes can be upsetting for a child. Many centers are short staffed, so that too few grownups must care for too many children. You will need to be vigilant about the quality of the center you choose.

For a parent, a day-care center can offer logistical problems. The facilities are often located far from home, meaning long morning and evening drives with a sleepy or tired child. The center's opening and closing schedule may not suit your own plans: Centers offer little flexibility in their hours. Most also ask that children who are sick stay home, which means that you must have backup care for sick days — or stay home with your child yourself. Last, you will need to resign yourself to the expense: The fees at good day-care centers are high. ❖

Finding and Evaluating Child-Care Services

Preliminary considerations

Before you begin your search for child care, you should decide how you feel about the issues that will be involved. You will want to match the day care to your child's needs — and yours.

The kind of day care you choose will be settled in part by your child's age and personality. Most people feel that infants do best with home care — either in your own house or at a family day-care home that can provide frequent, one-on-one, loving attention. Some day-care centers offer this, but they are difficult to find *(box, page 41)*. Toddlers, struggling for independence, also do best in an informal, homey situation. Most children of two and a half or three, however, are probably ready — even eager — for the extra stimulation a day-care center can provide.

Much depends on the child's personality. An easygoing young one with an optimistic outlook on life will readily adapt to new surroundings; she will get along with just about everyone and will find rules easy to follow. She will probably make herself at home at a center. The predictability of events in a day-care center and its range of activities also can be good for children who are easily frustrated, who cry frequently and who have difficulty adjusting to new routines. But shy, slow-to-warm children may have trouble settling in with a large group; to force such a child to make an adjustment too quickly would be unfair.

Among the practical matters to keep in mind as you start your search is location. It is less of an issue if the caregiver comes to your house, although you will want to consider how far she has to travel: A long morning trip is tiring and will make it harder for her to get to you on time; a long evening trip may make her reluctant to stay late on days when you must work late yourself.

When child care is outside your home, location assumes much greater importance. You want the best possible care for your child, but you do not want it so far away that you and your youngster spend hours riding in a car. A good rule is that day care should be no more than five to 10 minutes away from either your office or your home, if at all possible. Having the caregiver near the office means you can pick your child up quickly when your work is done — a help on days when you must work late and an advantage in case of emergencies. But having the caregiver nearer your home shortens the commute for your child.

Finally, of course, you must fit the day care to your budget. The cost will vary according to the area where you live, the type of care you choose and even your child's age. Care is most expensive in urban areas and in the Northeast and on the West Coast. In-home care usually costs somewhat more than center care — and several times what family day care costs. The price of

How to Interview a Prospective Caregiver

Interviewing a caregiver can be an exhausting experience. You must ask questions, listen, observe and respond almost simultaneously. Many parents find it helpful to prepare and review a list of questions before the actual interview takes place. The examples given here can help you formulate your own list of questions for a caregiver.

In-home caregiver

● What experience have you had taking care of children?

● What was your last job like?

● Why did you leave it?

● Are you planning to stay in this line of work for long?

● Have you had a medical checkup and chest X-rays recently?

● Do you drive? If not, how would you get to work?

● Do you smoke or drink?

● Would you be able to come early or stay late occasionally?

● Which religious holidays and other days would you need off each year?

● What kind of things do you like doing with children?

● How would you go about weaning a child from a bottle? Or toilet training a youngster?

● How do you believe children should be disciplined?

● Do you do housework? (Specify what jobs would be required.)

Family day-care provider

● What made you decide to open a family day-care home?

● Why have you decided to accept another child at this time?

● What do you find most difficult about raising children?

● What kinds of rewards and punishments do you use to discipline children?

● What is the daily routine for children under your care?

● Where do the children play and nap?

● What do you do when a child cries because she misses her mother or father?

● Do the children watch television? If so, which programs?

● What do you fix for lunches and snacks?

● What other members of your family will be in the household, and might they provide caregiving also?

● Do you provide backup care when you are sick?

● When do you usually take your vacation and for how long?

● What clothing or other equipment must I provide for my youngster to be left at your home?

Day-care center director

● What is your center's philosophy for caring for children?

● What is your center's philosophy about disciplining children?

● Is your day-care center affiliated with any religious group or other organization? How does this influence the kind of care offered at the center?

● Does the center have a formal educational program? If so, what are the components of that program?

● How many full-time children are at your center? How many part-time children?

● What is the adult-to-child ratio for infants, toddlers and preschoolers?

● What training and education is required of the staff?

● How many teachers have been on staff for more than one year?

● What is your policy about sick children coming to the center?

● Are parents expected to provide lunches and changes of clothing?

● Does the center have an active parent board that is involved in the operation of the program?

care usually is highest when your child is an infant — double what it will be after her first birthday.

It helps to remember, however, that you will get back some of the cost of your child's care as a credit on your federal income tax — and in some states on your state tax — at the end of each year. This is not a tax deduction, which is subtracted from your gross income: The credit is taken directly from the taxes you owe. How large the credit will be depends on your adjusted gross annual income. Your local Internal Revenue Service office or your tax accountant can give you detailed information.

When to start looking   It is true that day care is in high demand. Good in-home care is hard to find, and in large cities, many of the better family day-care homes and centers have long waiting lists. There are tales of couples who reserve places as soon as they learn they will be having a baby and of singles who put their names on waiting lists even before they have chosen marital partners.

These, of course, are worst-case stories. Still, the sooner you begin looking for day care, the better. Experts recommend that you start your search six months before you will be needing a caregiver. That will allow time for the telephone calls, interviews and visits to homes and centers that the process demands.

The first steps   A search for day care of any kind should begin with people you know. Ask everyone — relatives, neighbors, friends, co-workers, your child's pediatrician and anyone else you trust — for names of good caregivers. A neighbor's housekeeper, for instance, may have a friend who could work for you. Or if it is family day care that interests you, you should know that many of the best homes do not advertise, preferring instead word-of-mouth referrals.

If word of mouth does not produce good leads, you can turn to some of the many institutions and agencies that offer guides to child care. In-home caregivers, for instance, can often be found through state employment agencies — and at no fee to either employer or caregiver. In many cities, private employment agencies specialize in finding domestic help, including caregivers; there are even nanny placement services. All of these will be happy to help you, for a fee. Look in the classified phone directory under Employment Agencies or Child Care.

Another way to find an in-home caregiver is to advertise in the newspaper, in your community newsletter or on bulletin boards. Be very specific in the ad about your basic requirements. If it is imperative, for example, that the caregiver be a licensed driver or an expert swimmer or a nonsmoker or a person fluent in English, say so. If you are expecting house cleaning, say that, too.

If you are looking for family day care or for a day-care center, it is likely that there will be help nearby. Private centers are often in the telephone book under Child Care or Day

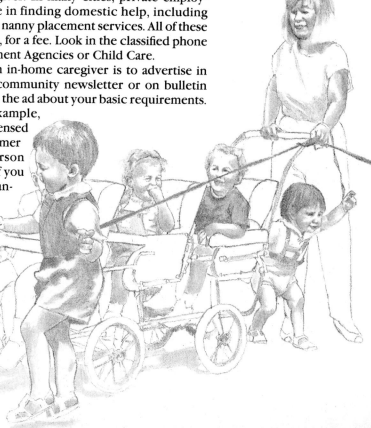

A caregiver should make provisions for outdoor exercise, whether in a fenced yard, a playground or a program of daily walks. Here, a caregiver keeps a group of two-year-olds safely in hand with a stroller and harnesses.

Nurseries. In addition, some communities have central child-care information and referral services that will give assistance; these will be listed under Social Service Organizations in the phone book. A call to a referral service should produce a list of family care homes and day-care centers in your neighborhood. And the service will help you sort through the options by giving current information about each place mentioned.

If your community lacks a referral service, your job will be a little more complicated. Begin by calling the agency that licenses day-care centers and homes in your area; call your state, county or municipal government information number for the name of the appropriate department. Most agencies can give you a list of the licensed facilities near your home or office. But they generally do not keep track of which facilities have openings, nor will they help distinguish good centers from average or bad ones: State laws forbid the agencies to provide detailed information about the quality of a particular center or home. The National Association for the Education of Young Children provides an accreditation procedure that helps to identify quality programs, although centers are not required to apply. But when a center displays its accreditation, it is an assurance of high standards. Armed with your list, you will have to find out the facts for yourself by telephoning, visiting and checking references.

When you are looking for child care, check with churches, synagogues, women's groups, nearby schools or colleges, and other community organizations. They often keep lists of people offering child care, and they may have information about the quality of particular caregivers, to help you narrow the field. It is useful, too, to read classified advertisements in the newspapers.

Telephone screening   Never settle for the first caregiver or center you hear about, no matter how convenient the situation seems to be or how highly it is recommended by a neighbor or friend: What works for a neighbor's child may not work for yours. You should always compare the options; once you have done so, you will feel more confident about your choice. And you will have leads to backup care, if the need should ever arise.

After you have developed a list of candidates, use the telephone to weed out those who are clearly unsuitable from those you would like to interview further. Your initial concerns will be very practical — location, flexibility of hours and cost.

The answers to these questions will help you narrow your list. You can narrow it further by getting other information, such as how much experience the caregiver has had or how long the center has been open. You can discover whether the caregiver will be available or has an opening in her home or center on the date you plan to return to work. And you should find out whether your child will fit in with the caregiver or center by giving particular details about him. You need to know whether the caregiver accepts infants, toddlers who are not toilet trained, children who require special diets, or whatever situation describes your child.

One attractive feature of family day care is that several family members, such as the father shown above or the older youngster opposite, can work and play with the children in addition to the primary caregiver. This makes the arrangement even more family-like and can provide extra entertainment for your child.

Finally, if the caregiver strikes you as a likely prospect and you plan to follow your call with an interview, ask for references. If the people you call raise doubts in your mind, you can cancel your visit and save yourself time.

You will get no more than a vague idea of a caregiver's personality and skill from the phone call. And do not be too quick to judge: Some people present a better image over the telephone than others. Only a personal interview will tell you what your candidate is really like.

The personal interview Whether you are planning to hire a nanny or enroll your child in a family day-care home or a day-care center, certain aspects of your interviews will remain the same. The interviews should be conducted wherever the child will be cared for — in your home for a nanny or a housekeeper, or at the day-care home or center. Your child should be with you for this talk: He needs to meet the caregiver, and the caregiver needs to meet him. So make sure to schedule your interviews for times of day when your child will be neither hungry nor tired. In order to get to know the caregiver, you should plan on a meeting of at least an hour.

A major reason for the interview is for you and the caregiver to get to know one another — for you to be clear about what you want and for her to be clear about what she can offer. You will want to hire someone you trust, of course, but you also want to be comfortable with that person, who will probably become a friend of yours as well as an employee. Do not expect to find someone who agrees with you on all aspects of child rearing

Instead, look for a person who respects your right to decide how your child is to be brought up and who is open to your approaches and ideas. Insofar as possible, you want your child to have a reasonable consistency of care.

It is best to begin the interview with casual, general questions. Does the caregiver have children of her own? What made her decide to take care of children? What does she like best about the job? Once the two of you are talking easily, you can move on to questions about more substantive issues, such as bottle weaning, toilet training and discipline. You will find that questions phrased in terms of real situations will get the most revealing answers. For example, you might ask what the caregiver would do if your child bit another child.

You should also ask any caregiver about daily routine, and you should be specific about what you want for your child in the way of meals, exercise, sleep and play projects. Does the caregiver believe in set times for snacks, lunch, naps and playing outdoors? Having a routine is a sign of good child care, although it should not be so rigid and organized that children are rushed and pushed from one activity to another.

You will need to discuss all the practical aspects of the day-care arrangement, such as hours, meals, vacations and sick days, rates and whether you will pay by the week or the month. Bring up any particular needs your child has — a special diet, for instance. Be especially candid with an in-home caregiver. You should discuss such topics as house rules, and if she lives in, whether she will eat with the family. And if you want her to be a housekeeper as well as a caregiver, you must be very specific about what kind of housework you expect. (For a list of questions to ask during an interview, see page 35.)

Last, you should remember that while you evaluate the caregiver, she is also assessing you. If you are too inflexible or too demanding, she will not want to work with you. You must be clear about which issues you stand firm on and on which issues you are willing to bend a little.

Evaluating the caregiver

The qualifications of caregivers vary widely — some very good ones have little formal training. However, you are not likely to find an outstanding caregiver who has not had a combination of personal experience with children and some formal training. For an in-home caregiver, for instance, you will probably want to hire someone experienced with children, who has a basic understanding of nutrition, who can drive a car and who has had a course in first aid. Depending on your circumstances, you may have other requirements. And you may expect different skills from the manager of a family day-care home or the director of a day-care center.

But the interview will give you insights beyond the basics about any caregiver, if you are a good observer. Let her do most of the talking and listen to her carefully. Does she seem intelligent? Does she fluster easily, or appear calm and capable? Is she enthusiastic and positive? Does she have a sense of humor?

You will particularly want to watch how the person responds to your child, or, if your child will be cared for outside your home, how she responds to the other children she cares for. Notice how she holds your infant or talks with your toddler. Does she appear comfortable and relaxed? How does she treat the other children who are around? How does she answer questions, help resolve conflicts, comfort hurt feelings? Do children come to her readily, or do they seem reserved or afraid?

Evaluating family day-care

As you interview and evaluate a family day-care provider, you should also be examining the home where your child will be staying: Its condition will tell you quite a lot about the atmosphere and kind of care the home provides. You should always tour the house and yard, observing them carefully.

A family day-care home should be both childproof and child oriented: safety latches on the appropriate cabinets; breakable objects out of a child's reach; toys, games, books, crayons and

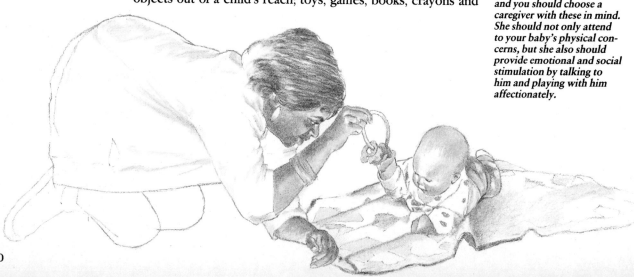

Infants have special needs, and you should choose a caregiver with these in mind. She should not only attend to your baby's physical concerns, but she also should provide emotional and social stimulation by talking to him and playing with him affectionately.

The Special Needs of Infants and Toddlers

Center care for children younger than three is difficult to find, largely for economic reasons: Infants and toddlers require a high adult-child ratio, and large staffs are expensive.

But a high adult-child ratio is necessary if caregivers are to meet the special needs of infants and toddlers. An infant must be fed when she is hungry, changed when she is wet, and above all, cuddled and talked to frequently and lovingly. Studies have shown that most adults cannot provide this kind of attention if they are caring for more than three babies at a time.

Toddler care is also very demanding. Toddlers are usually quick on the move, getting into and exploring everything. In addition, a toddler's mood may well shift rapidly and without warning, from compliance to rejection, from helplessness to independence. Toddlers therefore require the firm, kind and almost constant guidance of understanding and watchful adults.

Keep these needs in mind when looking for infant and toddler care at a center. First, make sure the day-care environment you choose is safe and comfortable. Babies should have strong, sturdy cribs to sleep in, located in a separate sleeping room. Other equipment — high chairs, baby swings, strollers and baby seats — should also be in good repair, and gates should be in front of unsupervised stairways and doorways. Play areas should be large enough to allow crawling babies to explore comfortably. All potentially dangerous objects should be out of sight and out of reach. Look for comfortable adult-size chairs, particularly rocking chairs, indicating that the babies are held frequently. If you see babies lying in cribs with bottles propped in their mouths, be wary. Not only is propping bottles dangerous for babies, who can easily choke when drinking, but it also denies them the physical closeness and social interaction so important in feedings.

Babies — even very young infants — need the mental and social stimulation of other people and should not be confined to their cribs or playpens while awake. A good caregiver will remove a baby from her crib as soon as she awakens, talk to her and engage her in some sort of playful activity.

Make sure the center has enough toys and equipment to keep a baby or toddler occupied and interested. The toys should also be appropriate for the age of the children. For infants, there should be colorful mobiles, brightly colored pictures on the walls and toys such as rattles to explore with their hands. Older babies and toddlers need a wider variety of toys and a great deal of indoor play space. They need small structures, such as padded stairs, to climb over and tunnel into; many of the better day-care centers provide large indoor tiled areas where toddlers can run, dance and ride tricycles.

Following are some points to consider when evaluating an infant-toddler day-care program:

● *Do caregivers spend enough time talking and playing with individual children, and does each child have one person who is her main caregiver?* Throughout the early years of life, a child needs to establish a stable relationship with someone who is especially concerned about her as an individual.

● *Does the day-care center have a quiet and peaceful place where children can have quiet time by themselves, away from the noise and demands of other children?*

● *Is aggressive and self-centered behavior dealt with in a swift but constructive manner?* A good caregiver assists in the process of teaching a youngster that other children have feelings that should be respected.

other materials for children where small hands can readily retrieve and use them. The toys should be suited to the ages of the children and should stimulate as well as entertain. Some of the play area should be carpeted, and the rooms should be warm and well ventilated. Ask to see where the children nap, to make sure that cots and cribs are safe, clean and comfortable.

The house should be clean and well kept — but not immaculate. An overly tidy house may mean that the caregiver is spending more time housekeeping than with the children. It is all right if one or two rooms are off-limits. But in general, they should have free run of the house, just as they would at home.

You should also examine the yard and other areas where children will play outdoors. How much space do they have? Is it fenced? Are there trees for shade? Are the riding toys, sandboxes and other play equipment sturdy and safe?

A visit to a day-care center will be a lengthy one. Plan on spending half an hour with the center's director, 15 minutes with the teacher of the class your child will be entering and at least an hour observing the children in their program. Eliminate from your list any center that discourages long visits or that will not allow unannounced shorter observation periods. Try to meet

Where Play Is Serious Business

The childhood lament, "There's nothing to do," is rarely heard at a good child-care center. A quality center offers daylong opportunities for children to do what they do best: play. Far from being an idle pursuit, children's play is the medium through which they learn.

As youngsters play, they satisfy curiosity with independent exploration and gain feedback from trial-and-error efforts. Through make-believe, they come to grips with the things that overwhelm or confuse them — a fear of ghosts, a parent's scolding or perhaps a puzzlement about how the doctor does his job.

You can recognize a day-care program that provides quality play by its flexibility and attentiveness to individual needs. The caregiver should have a goal for each child based on his developmental level. Activities should be initiated by the child as well as by an adult.

Be sure the center you choose alternates quiet times with energetic activities, outdoor with indoor play, structured play with free play. Check whether games for developing small-muscle skills, such as puzzles, are interspersed with games for large-muscle skills, such as Simon says. Creative projects — art and blocks, for example — should take place largely through free play. And look for replicas of everyday articles, such as dress-up clothes or kitchen equipment, as signs that the staff recognizes the need children have to act out adult roles.

Dressing her doll, this little girl creates an imaginary family in which she is the mother. As she mimics her own mother's speech and actions, she reaches some understanding of behavior that may have puzzled her.

Concentrating on her task, a child spins the wheel of an overturned tricycle and tightens invisible bolts with imaginary wrenches. In her make-believe play, she experiments with possibilities and arrives at solutions.

As she explores shapes and colors, this girl enjoys her mastery over raw materials and delights in the freedom to create patterns. Praise from her caregivers will bolster her confidence and ready her for the next task.

The symbols that make up reading and writing become familiar to a boy pounding away on an old typewriter. Using different fingers to punch the keys, he is also developing fine-motor skills.

Fitting the cylinders into the pegboard, this youngster is absorbing information about geometric shapes and spatial relationships. His trial-and-error matching prepares him for more difficult problem solving later.

Usually more than other caregivers, day-care centers provide events for children that help them learn and grow. One such event might be a visit from a firefighter, as shown on these pages, with a talk on safety and even a chance to try on the firefighter's gear.

first with the center's director. She should show you the center's license and offer you other written material that outlines such items as hours, fees, and the responsibilities and privileges of both the center and the parents. You should also ask to see a weekly lunch menu, so that you can be sure meals are nutritious.

The director should provide information about the center's ratio of adults to children and about the staff's training and experience. Opinions vary as to what a good ratio should be; in general, you should look for at least one adult for each of the following groups of children: every four babies, every six to eight toddlers, every 10 to 12 three- and four-year-olds, and every 15 to 20 five-year-olds. As for training: Ask how many staff members have been trained in child development and early childhood education — there should be at least one such caregiver in each classroom. Try to find out if most of the workers have been there for a reasonable length of time, at least a year. Staff stability is a positive sign.

When the director has answered your basic questions about the center, you will be ready to talk with and observe the class-

room teacher. Listen and look for the same traits and skills that you would look for in an in-home or family caregiver. Is the teacher enthusiastic and energetic? Does she appear to like her job? When she speaks with a child, does she look directly at the child or glance around the room, preoccupied with other matters? Does she kneel down to talk with children on their own level? Also watch to see whether the teacher makes an effort to be with as many children as possible during the time you observe her. If there is a withdrawn child in the classroom, does she make an attempt to draw him out?

Take a good look at the activities, materials and overall environment of the center. Although you want a center that is clean and relatively neat, remember that fancy carpeting and expensive equipment bear little if any relationship to the quality of a particular program. The center should have adequate space (and time on its daily schedule) for rests and naps as well as for activities. The outside play area should be of a comfortable size and securely fenced; its equipment, like that of a family care home, should be sturdy and safe. The center should also have a safe place for delivering and picking up children.

Finally, give yourself a general picture of the life of the place. The toys and materials should be plentiful and appropriate to the children's ages. Activities should be varied, and there should be a good balance between structured activities and free choice. Group programs should be kept to a minimum, with children free not to participate if they find the play too demanding or overwhelming. Above all, watch the children — who will be your own child's companions. They should be playing and working happily.

Trusting your judgment

When it comes down to making the final decision about which center or caregiver to choose, trust your judgment. You should feel comfortable with a nanny or housekeeper and welcome at the family day-care home or center you select. And you should feel that your ideas, suggestions and questions are welcome.

Ask yourself which day-care arrangement you would prefer if you were a child again. Observe your child's reactions to the caregivers he meets. If he is old enough, ask him for his opinion about the people and places he visited.

Above all, base your choice of day care on merits, not on convenience. The center down the street may be tempting, but if its rooms are dark and its caregivers overworked, it is not the environment in which you want to place your child. ⁙

A Community of Children

Whatever the pros and cons of day care for infants, once your child has reached the age of two and a half to three years, you are clearly promoting her social development by exposing her to a group of her peers on a regular basis. Young children acquire social skills — like all of their new abilities — through practice and trial and error. And while staying home with mother has its own advantages, the kinds of social interaction shown on the following pages are possible only in a community of other children. Many stay-at-home mothers choose to enroll their children in organized play programs just to create such group opportunities; regular day care provides this benefit automatically.

Perhaps owing to the enormous influence of the Swiss psychologist Jean Piaget, child-development experts long contended that toddlers were too egocentric and unaware of those around them to interact with other children in meaningful ways — let alone learn from one another. More recent researchers have moved away from that assumption. They note that although the interactions of toddlers are immature, these behaviors are in their own way quite complex and may be seen as meaningful steps toward more mature

social behavior. By the time a child enters kindergarten, she must be operating at a certain level of social competency in order to get a good start in school. Day care presents continuing opportunities for a youngster to practice the social skills that she needs.

The best kind of group-care setting enables a youngster to have a good time while learning how to get along with others. In her daily dealings with other girls and boys, she experiments with different ways of resolving conflicts. She learns to enjoy give and take, to share toys and ideas, to take an interest in the people around her. This in turn leads her to invest herself emotionally in other children — the key to developing friendships. It is up to the care provider to maximize the social benefits in the way the children's program is arranged and planned. Toddlers need frequent guidance when learning how to interact with their peers, and the caregiver is usually the person on hand to mediate and serve as a model for positive behavior. A good instructor gently steers your youngster away from anger, resentment or frustration and gently nudges her instead toward discussion, sharing and compassion.

Self-Esteem through Sharing

Handled properly, the time-honored exercise called show and tell bolsters a child's self-esteem by letting her see that her teachers and peers value what she has to say. Nowadays, many child-care instructors dispense with the structure of show and tell as a formal exercise but preserve its spirit by staying watchful for moments throughout the day when children obviously have something to share, and then inviting them to express themselves.

Learning to Listen and Observe

Group exercise reinforces the essential lesson about following instructions in a very positive way. This is a situation in which every child is able to succeed: There are lots of ways to reach for the ceiling or touch your toes, and each child finds his own way of doing it. The children learn to follow directions by listening to the teacher and watching her example, but also by observing each other.

Practicing Responsible Behavior

Most good child-care centers strictly enforce the rule that children must pick up after themselves. The object is to instill a sense of responsibility toward the group, toward the classroom that they all share and toward the toys or materials that the children enjoy. Picking up also becomes a lesson in the benefits of working together. Sometimes the instructor will team a child who is strong at following through on responsibilities with one who is weak in this area and needs a positive example to follow.

Appreciating Differences

One of the first lessons of spending time outside the home is that not everyone looks, talks or acts the same way. In fact, children learn much about their own identities by perceiving the differences between themselves and others. A child-care program that includes youngsters from diverse cultural and economic backgrounds will give your child a valuable head start toward understanding, accepting and appreciating people who are different from her and her family.

Opportunities to Be Self-Sufficient

Trading the protective environment of the family for the company of peers, most children are eager to take on new challenges — including trying out grown-up roles that they only observe at home. The instinct for self-sufficiency is encouraged in a group-care setting by do-it-yourself policies at the coat rack, in the lavatory and at the lunch table. Even if he is not always able to succeed at a particular feat, such as pouring juice from a thermos, your youngster learns that the important thing is to try.

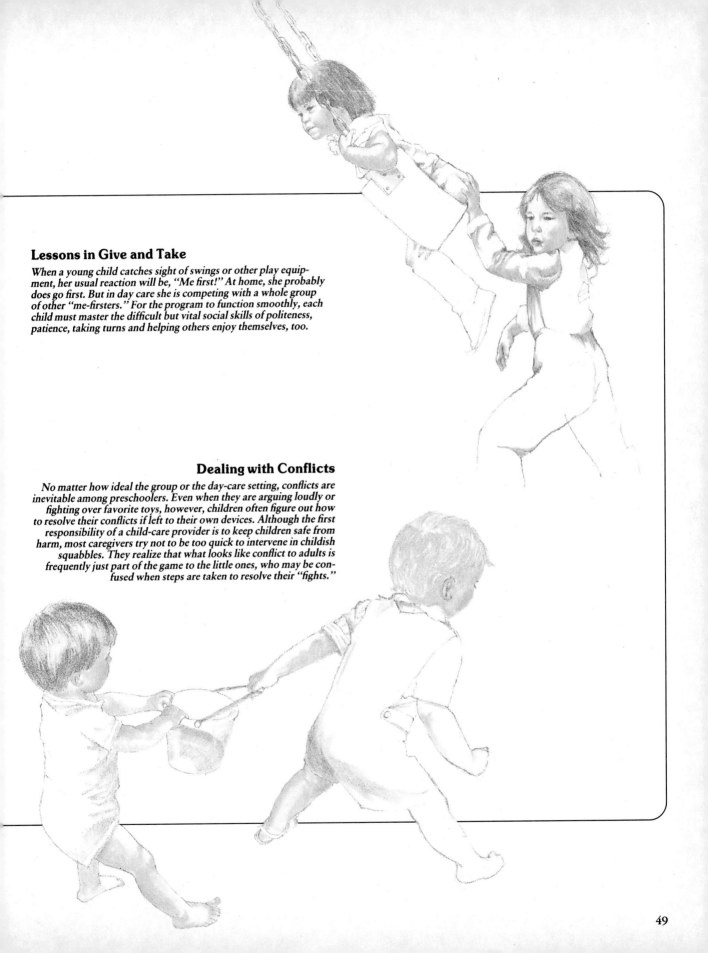

Lessons in Give and Take

When a young child catches sight of swings or other play equipment, her usual reaction will be, "Me first!" At home, she probably does go first. But in day care she is competing with a whole group of other "me-firsters." For the program to function smoothly, each child must master the difficult but vital social skills of politeness, patience, taking turns and helping others enjoy themselves, too.

Dealing with Conflicts

No matter how ideal the group or the day-care setting, conflicts are inevitable among preschoolers. Even when they are arguing loudly or fighting over favorite toys, however, children often figure out how to resolve their conflicts if left to their own devices. Although the first responsibility of a child-care provider is to keep children safe from harm, most caregivers try not to be too quick to intervene in childish squabbles. They realize that what looks like conflict to adults is frequently just part of the game to the little ones, who may be confused when steps are taken to resolve their "fights."

Agreements and Other Paper Work

Continuity is the key to a day-care arrangement that is good for your child. A comfortable routine with a caregiver and a minimum of disturbing changes are what he needs for healthy growth and development. So you will need to take steps from the moment you choose a caregiver to ensure that your arrangement is a long and happy one.

A child-care agreement
To minimize disagreements, both you and your caregiver should be clear from the outset about your expectations; and you should put those expectations in writing in the form of an agreement that defines duties and responsibilities for you both *(box, right)*. Such an agreement is not a legal contract. It is simply a formal means of understanding each other.

If your caregiver is to come to your home, you will be the one who drafts the agreement. Describe your expectations in detail: The agreement should cover practical matters as well as more subjective issues. If you want the caregiver to take your child outdoors every day, note it; if you do not want her friends to visit during working hours, put that down, too; if you do not want your child to play with war-related toys, make sure the contract includes a statement to that effect.

Some family day-care providers — especially those sponsored by a network or association — have their own ready-made agreements. But you still should sit down with the caregiver and negotiate any points of concern. Remember that family day care is provided in the caregiver's home, not in yours: Special considerations you can reasonably ask will be somewhat limited.

Day-care centers also have their own agreement forms, which they will ask you to read and sign. Again, if the center's agreement does not cover all the matters that are important to you, feel free to suggest changes.

Other paperwork
For the sake of your child's health and safety, your caregiver needs to have quite a lot of information about you. You should provide the person or the center with a parent-information card that lists your work and home telephone numbers, your home and work addresses, the name, address and telephone number of your child's physician, your child's health insurance number and any other information that might be needed in an emergency. If your child is allergic to penicillin, for example, you should include that information on the card.

Day-care centers and some family day-care homes will also ask you to give them a record of your child's medical history. The health record enables a center to make sure that your child is up-to-date on all immunizations, and it also provides a helpful record of which diseases and illnesses your child may be susceptible to, such as hay fever.

Also provide your caregiver or day-care center with a signed medical release form. This form authorizes your caregiver to seek treatment for your child if there is an emergency and you cannot be reached. Usually the form contains a simple statement, such as "I, (your name), give (the caregiver or center's name) the authority to make emergency medical decisions regarding the care of my child, (your child's name), when I cannot be reached by telephone." Sign the statement. Although it may be discomforting to sign away your power to make emergency medical decisions concerning your child, you should understand that doctors and hospitals are sometimes legally unable to provide care without authorized consent. Life-threatening accidents can happen, and it is important that your caregiver have the authority to get treatment for your child in your absence. ❖

An Agreement for In-Home Care

In-home care allows you the greatest degree of control over the details involved in your child's daily care. The agreement you draw up can include virtually anything that you consider important to your youngster's well-being and the employer-employee relationship. Here are some items you should consider:

- the hours and days that the caregiver is to work
- salary, minus any amount withheld

for FICA and FUTA; pay for overtime, holidays, vacation and sick leave
- when and how the caregiver's salary is to be paid
- procedures for evaluating the working agreement and the caregiver's salary at intervals
- amount of notice and salary required to end the relationship
- cooking, housekeeping chores or chauffeuring duties the caregiver is expected to perform, and whether she will be paid extra

- emergency arrangements in the event of bad weather, illness or accidents
- your expectations concerning the caregiver's visitors, personal phone calls and use of television and radio during working hours
- guidelines for your youngster's mealtimes, naps, outdoor play and television viewing, as well as safety precautions and discipline
- medications that must be administered to your child, or special restrictions to enforce

Agreements for Family Care and Day-Care Centers

Although your family care provider or day-care center may have a standard form for you to sign, you may have additional concerns or requests to bring up and negotiate at the time you enroll your child. Following are some points to consider:

- the hours and days that care will be provided
- regular fees and expenses for field trips or other extras
- when and how fees are to be paid
- payment policies for vacation, days

missed, late pickup and other special circumstances
- arrangements for substitute care in case of the caregiver's vacation or illness or an emergency situation
- policies concerning the care of a sick youngster
- procedures for changing or terminating the arrangement
- the caregiver-child ratio
- transportation arrangements
- list of persons other than parents who are authorized to pick up the child from the day-care home or center

- what meals and snacks are provided by the caregiver or center
- what educational and recreational activities, toys, play equipment and infant furniture are provided by the day-care home or center
- food, clothing or equipment that must be brought from home
- instructions concerning your child's diet, medications or restrictions on activities
- policies regarding health insurance and medical treatment if needed in case of emergency

Making Day Care Work

Preparing your child

Separating from you is likely to be distressing for your child, but you can ease the pangs — and smooth her transition into day care — by the way you prepare her for the change.

At every age, there will be preliminaries. If your child is an infant who has been breast-feeding, for example, you will need to introduce her to a bottle several weeks before she begins day care. Older children — those at least 18 months of age — need explanations in advance about what day care will mean. Take your child aside some days before care is to begin. Calmly and confidently tell her that a caregiver will be coming to your house to play with her, or that she will be going to a day-care home or center to play with other children. Say that you will be working during the day and that every day after your work is done, you will return to her. Repeat this explanation until you feel sure that your child understands it.

An attitude of confidence

Your attitude during these conversations — and during the entire separation process — is important. You should exude confidence and the belief that things will be all right, because even very young children are sensitive to their parents' feelings. Studies have shown that the babies of mothers who are apprehensive about leaving their children make a poorer adjustment to day care than do babies of mothers who are positive and confident.

Even the most confident parents, however, may have a child who is especially shy and slow to adjust to unfamiliar people and strange situations. Such children may need extra preparation for day care. For children who seem unusually resistant, preliminary visits are often reassuring. If you have hired an in-home caregiver, arrange for her to visit you and your child several times before you return to work. Or, if the child is going away from home, take her for visits to her new day-care home or center a week or so before she is scheduled to begin. Let her play just long enough to make her eager to return.

The first day

When the big day arrives, arrange your schedule so that you feel calm and unhurried. Give yourself plenty of time to dress your child and to have a leisurely breakfast and a few quiet moments together before meeting with or driving to the caregiver. Above all, do not rush your child: Hurrying can create nervousness and unnecessary insecurity.

You will probably find in your preliminary discussions that your family day-care provider or day-care center director has a preferred routine — based on long experience — for handling the initial separation. She may want you to stay with your child

Coping with Separation

66 When I left Andy at a preschool center, he hugged my leg and cried even though I did what the director advised: 'Be firm about leaving, tell him you'll come back, kiss him good-by and turn around and leave.' As a divorced parent, I felt the need to do more. I explained many times that I didn't want to leave him but that I had to work so we could have food and toys and a home. Andy's three, but even a very young child can begin to realize what life is about; I didn't want him to think I left him just to get rid of him. He seemed to understand what I was saying and be helped by it. 99

66 I'm lucky to have many relatives who live nearby. From the time my children were infants, they stayed with one family member or another for several days at a time — as often as twice a month. So by the time I entered them in day care at two and a half, they were used to being in various group situations without us, and they never cried at all. 99

66 When Keith changed to a prekindergarten group, he began clinging just the way he had when he started day care. But this time we hired a sixth grader to take him to school. She comes when we leave for work, plays with Keith at home, then walks him to school and takes him to his class. He enjoys playing with her so much that he doesn't mind when we leave. 99

66 We started out leaving Melanie at a day-care center when she was eight months old, and she cried so much I just couldn't take it. So we decided to have an au pair live with us. But Mellie still would cry and cling to me as I left. Soon, the au pair was able to distract her with food and a toy. A while later, I noticed she would have a special smile or hug for the au pair. While I was relieved to see how well they were getting along, I found myself feeling jealous: 'She's my baby — that smile should be for me.' 99

66 Three months after Peter was born, I had to go to work, and I put my baby in the sitter's arms expecting an outcry. But there was not a peep that day — and no crying later on. Maybe three months is the perfect age to start day care, so he can adjust to it before he is old enough for anxiety to set in. Or maybe my sitter just has a special way with children. 99

66 Before my two-year-old began day care, a caregiver from the center visited my home to talk about separation anxiety, explaining that children need to know that they will be cared for. When I started to leave him at the center, he clung to me like a monkey and I had to peel him off. On the fourth day, he stopped crying, and he hasn't cried since. I believed, from the beginning, he would stop crying quickly. The main effect of the visit was to reassure me about how responsible and dedicated the staff was; I think my confidence reassured my son. 99

for an hour or even all day the first day; on the other hand, she may want you to make the break soon after you and your child arrive. As a general guideline, staying with your child at least an hour the first day is a good idea, and you may need to stay longer if your child is between eight and 15 months old — the age when babies are most resistant to separations.

This period with your child should be as relaxed as possible. Take time to introduce him to the caregiver; if your child is going to family day care or a day-care center, introduce him to the other children, too. Do not try to force him to play with anyone, however. Lead him to the toys and encourage him to do something specific, such as, "Build a block tower for Mommy." Make sure the project does not require your participation: You want to be as inconspicuous as possible. Your departure will be easier if he is playing independently before you leave.

Leave-taking No matter how carefully you prepare your child and yourself, you may find the moment when you rise to leave particularly

painful. Your departure — the first stage of separation — may well include your child's crying, screaming, clinging to your leg, hitting the caregiver and otherwise letting you know how thoroughly unhappy she is with the idea of your leaving her.

The way to handle the situation is swiftly and calmly. Long good-byes tend to give young children confusing information and make the separation more difficult. So simply tell your child that you must go to work now and that you will return for her later. Describe when you will be back, using a reference your child will understand: "I'll pick you up right after your nap," or "Daddy will come for you right before dinnertime." Never slip out without telling your child you are leaving: That is the way to destroy her trust in you.

And resist the temptation to go back and give a wailing child one more reassuring hug. That will only encourage her to cry when you leave, in hopes of getting you back. Although many parents find it difficult to believe, most children stop weeping within minutes after their parents walk out the door.

In new situations or during times of particular stress, the separation from you at the beginning of the day is apt to make your child anxious. When this happens, ease his way by staying with him for a while as he warms up to his caregiver (left); watch while he gets involved with a game or toys (below). Then say good-by and leave. A good caregiver will provide extra comfort if the child cries (opposite).

Experts call the second stage of separation absence, meaning the time you and your child actually are apart, and there are several ways you can ease her initial anxiety about it. If she is going to a home or center, take something from home to leave with her — a favorite toy, a blanket — to ease the transition between your home and the new surroundings. A photograph of you or of you and your youngster together can be especially reassuring; in fact, many day-care centers ask parents to send photographs, which they post on special bulletin boards for all the children to see. Or you may wish to telephone your child during the first weeks of day care. This can be a good thing — as long as your child does not find your faraway voice more upsetting than comforting.

Reunion
The final stage of day care — the reunion at the end of the day when the child returns to his parents — can be an un-

happy surprise. Instead of a youngster joyful to greet you, you may find a child as teary and tense as when you left. Particularly during his first few weeks of adjustment to day care, your child may react to your return with tears, whining and babyish displays, no matter what his age. A one-year-old, for example, may demand to be held and may scream every time his father tries to put him down; a four-year-old may declare that he no longer remembers how to put on his coat and insist that his mother do it for him. Some children, on the other hand, ignore their parents or react to them with indifference.

All of this behavior is a natural expression of your child's anger at you for leaving. To dispel his resentment, greet him affectionately; establish physical contact by picking him up or hugging him. And give him your complete attention. Talk to him exclusively. If he is old enough, ask him about his day and listen attentively to his answers. If he has a long story, let him tell it.

And try to remain as relaxed as you can. Just as you want to avoid rushing your child to day care, you want to avoid rushing him home again. Children need more time than adults do to make the emotional adjustment to both separation and reunion.

Making a permanent adjustment

Adjusting to day care can take a child a few days or a few weeks, depending on the child's personality and on how her parents feel about leaving her in someone else's care. Relaxed, easygoing children adjust much more quickly to day care than do those with more timid personalities.

In general, you can expect your child to become reasonably reconciled to the new arrangement by about her 10th full day of day care. At that point, she should have begun to form an emotional attachment to her caregiver and should be seeking out the caregiver's attention, rather than shying away from it. If the caregiver comes to your home, your child should be eager to start playing as soon as you have left. Or if she goes to a family home or a center, she should be joining into play quickly after arriving. She should also be calmer when you say good-by to her in the morning and happier when you greet her in the evening.

Do not be surprised, however, if your child takes longer than two weeks to adjust to day care. Nor should you become alarmed if she suddenly begins to exhibit behavior that is immature for her age. A toilet-trained three-year-old, for ex-

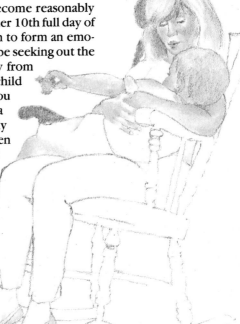

ample, may begin wetting her pants, or a four-year-old may redis-cover how comforting sucking a thumb can be. For children, such regressive behavior is a common reaction to stress; it ends when the stress — in this case, the adjustment to separation — ends. If the behavior seems excessive, however, or if it goes on for longer than a few months, you and your caregiver may wish to rethink how you can make the adjustment period easier for your youngster.

Parent and caregiver

Communications between you and your child's caregiver will have a profound effect on how your youngster adjusts to day care. From the start, you should aim for an open and friendly relationship, one that is based on trust and mutual respect. You can begin to build such a relationship by treating your child's caregiver as a co-worker — someone whose opinions and viewpoints you respect — rather than as a servant who is there simply to do your bidding. Always meet the terms of your day-care agreement; for example, be prompt about payments and about coming home or picking up your child at the end of the day. And you should praise your caregiver when praise is due. If she succeeds where you have failed — such as in get-ting your son to eat vegetables or to use the potty chair — then be sure to thank her. Everyone appreciates acknowledg-ment of a job well done.

Another key to a good parent-caregiver relationship is fre-quent and frank conversation. You should feel free to discuss all aspects of your child's personality and welfare, from his dis-like of peanut-butter-and-jelly sandwiches to his fear of another youngster at the day-care home or center. Tell your caregiver from the start of the arrangement that you would like to talk with her regularly about your child's progress. You may even wish to put into your day-care agreement when and how often these discussions will take place.

Scheduled conferences

Most matters can be discussed briefly and informally during the times you are picking up and delivering your child. But more major concerns — such as a disagreement between you and the caregiver about when to introduce solid foods to your infant or when to toilet train your toddler — should be discussed at a specially planned meeting time. If time and other constraints make it impossible for you to meet face-to-face regularly, you can arrange to confer over the phone instead.

Day-care centers usually schedule quarterly or biannual con-ferences with parents. Never hesitate to request additional conferences if you feel them necessary. You may also wish to schedule a special visit to the center to observe firsthand how your child is doing.

Be sure your communication with your child's caregiver is two-way. She needs information from you as much as you need it from her. If your daughter has slept poorly the night before, tell the caregiver; she will then be able to adjust naptime to make up for the lost sleep. Or if your son is worried because his grandmother is ill, explain the situation to your caregiver; she can then be prepared to give your son the extra comforting he may need to deal with his worry.

A written record To keep the communication channels between you and your caregiver fully open, you may wish to establish a written log in which both of you record daily observations of your child. Such a log is especially helpful if your youngster goes to a day-care center, where more than one person may be caring for her. In the morning, for example, you might put in an entry such as this: "Jenny was sneezing a lot at breakfast. It may be her allergies acting up again. Please call me if the symptoms persist through the day so I can arrange to get her medicine on my way home from work this afternoon." Or at the end of the day, your caregiver might write: "Jonathan drank readily from a cup today at lunch. Only a few spills! You may want to try a cup again at dinner." Although it may seem like a lot of extra work, a written log need take only two or three minutes of your time each day. And you will have the satisfaction of knowing that you and your caregiver are providing your child with continuous and consistent care.

Avoiding rivalry It is natural for a parent to feel jealous of her child's caregiver from time to time — when your child accidentally calls his caregiver "Mommy," for example, or when he asks to spend extra time with her. Try not to interpret such slips of the tongue or shows of affection as signs that your child is more attached to the caregiver than to you. Although children can become very fond of their caregivers, their primary emotional attachments are to their mothers and fathers *(pages 12-13)*.

Feelings of rivalry between parent and caregiver can be especially strong when the caregiver is a relative. In such a situation, even minor disagreements can be taken personally and can lead to deep resentments. A grandmother who brought up an entire family on white bread, for example, may feel that her son's request to feed her three-year-old granddaughter only whole-wheat bread is a slap at her own past efforts as a mother. The son, on the other hand, may resent the fact that his mother does not respect his wishes.

If you have an open and friendly relationship with your caregiver, feelings of jealousy and rivalry are less likely to become a problem. Never undermine your caregiver's authority or minimize her importance in front of your child. If you disagree with something your caregiver is doing — such as giving your child candy during the day — raise the issue privately with your caregiver, not with your child. Children get confused when they are caught in the middle of a dispute — especially when the dispute is over their care — and they may respond by becoming resistant to adults.

Communicating with your child

If your child is old enough, try to set aside some time each evening to ask him about what he did during the day. Ask specific questions, phrased in a way to elicit more than a "yes" or "no": "What kinds of games did you play outside today?" "Can you tell me the story you heard this afternoon at storytime?" "Which friends did you play with today?" Such a discussion not only provides you with clues about how well your child is adjusting to day care, but it also lets your child know you think of him even when you are away.

Many children love to aggravate their parents by answering "I don't know" to all questions posed to them. They enjoy the sense of independence and power that comes from knowing something their parents do not. You can sometimes break through this silence by offering to exchange details of your day for details of your child's. For example, you might describe to your youngster what you ate for lunch, then ask him to tell you what he had. Or you could tell him a story you heard and then ask him to tell you one that he heard. Such exchanges not only help satisfy a child's natural curiosity, they also give your youngster the message that you consider his daily activities as important as yours.

When your child does talk about his day, you should not take everything he says literally. Many young children have imaginations that are more vivid than their memories. One three-year-old youngster at a family day-care home, for example, told his mother and father that he took his naps in a bathtub, although his day-care provider always put him down to sleep in a very soft (and very dry) bed.

Of course, this does not mean you should disregard every outlandish-sounding story your child tells you about his day-

care experiences. The exaggerated stories told by children often reflect a hidden truth. For example, if your child repeatedly, although inaccurately, insists that he is never permitted to play games outside with the other children at his day-care center, it may mean that something is happening on the playground that is troubling him. Perhaps the outside games are too rough for him, or he feels excluded from the play. Talk to your child, and then call your caregiver to see if there is a hidden truth behind a particular tale.

As your child adjusts to day care, take the time to get involved in her world. This may mean attending a father's day event, as shown here, or volunteering to help with the center's work in one way or another.

Getting involved If your youngster is cared for away from home, you will find that one of the best ways of ensuring that her experiences are happy is to become actively involved in what goes on at the day-care center or home. Some centers have monthly parent-caregiver meetings — similar to parent-teacher meetings in schools — in which broad issues of mutual interest to parents and caregivers are discussed, such as school policies or educational programs. Be sure to attend social events as well — any picnics or parties organized by your day-care provider or your day-care center's staff. Not only will your attendance please your child, but it will also give you a chance to meet the parents of the children your child plays with all day.

You should also volunteer for as many activities as you can find the time and energy for. You may wish to become directly active in learning experiences at your child's day-care home or center by sharing a particular skill or hobby — anything from bassoon playing to bird calling.

Some parents enjoy stopping by once a week to read a story to their child's class or to assist in an art project. Or you may wish to provide other services to your youngster's center, such as writing or editing the center's newsletter or becoming involved in raising funds for new playground equipment or other needed projects. Some day-care centers also have parent advisory boards that play very active roles in the running of the centers; ask how you can become involved. ❖

When Problems Arise

Day care does not always run smoothly. Problems sometimes occur that can make the going quite bumpy — your youngster gets sick, your caregiver retires or moves to a different town, or something happens that threatens your child's physical or emotional well-being. But you can prepare for such happenings. By being aware of what can go wrong with day care, you can take steps to ensure that things go right again as quickly as possible.

Medical concerns
In family day care or at a center, where several children are together, the risk of illness is greater than it is in your home. Your child can catch — or spread — more than influenza and chicken pox. Other common contagious illnesses include diarrhea, strep throat, impetigo and conjunctivitis. Parasites, such as head lice, can also be easily passed from child to child.

Just a few germs on a hand or toy can spread an infection. Diseases of the intestinal tract, such as diarrhea, are spread by infected stool's getting onto hands and, from there, into food or onto objects that are then placed in the mouth; respiratory ailments are spread through coughs, sneezes and runny noses.

Although the risk of catching a contagious illness cannot be entirely eliminated from a day-care setting, it can be minimized with good hygiene practices. Check to make sure that caregivers at your child's day-care center wash their hands frequently — always after changing a diaper or wiping a nose, and before preparing or serving a meal. Diapers should be changed at an easily cleaned location separate from the general play area. Toys should be periodically disinfected, and soft, cloth-covered toys likely to be mouthed should not be available to the youngest children. You and your caregiver must cooperate to teach your child good personal hygiene. Make sure he washes his hands after using the bathroom and before eating. Instruct him at an early age how to properly wipe his nose — or at least not to fight when an adult wipes it.

Your responsibilities
For your child's safety and the safety of other children in his day-care arrangement, you should make sure he is adequately immunized. In fact, most states require children in licensed day-care facilities to be up-to-date on their shots. In addition to immunizing your child, you should take the responsibility for

A step to stand on and a helping hand encourage this child to wash after using the bathroom. Attention to cleanliness and to teaching proper hygiene are characteristics you should look for in any caregiver.

notifying your caregiver if your child has been exposed to someone who has a contagious disease, such as chicken pox.

Above all, you have the responsibility of recognizing when your child is too ill to go to his day-care home or center. You must then keep him at home; and you should insist that the parents of his playmates do the same when their children are sick. In general, a child should stay home if he has a fever or diarrhea; if he is vomiting or feeling nauseated; if he has a severe stomachache, earache, headache or other pain; if he has an unexplained rash; or if he complains of feeling weak and unwell. Be honest with your caregiver about your child's symptoms. She will become angry and resentful if the baby you dropped off with a "slight tummy ache" is actually unable to keep any food down.

Backup care   Because it is inevitable that your child will become ill from time to time, you should have backup plans for her care. Parents who have an in-home caregiver or family day care should also have contingency plans for those days when the caregiver becomes ill. You may opt to have yourself or your spouse stay home with the child. A few employers permit their employees to take paid personal days when their young ones are sick; most parents cope with the situation, however, by using vacation time or sick leave.

For those days when you cannot stay home from work, you need to prepare a list of backup sitters who are willing to step in at a moment's notice. Obvious choices are relatives or close friends who are not working; talk to them beforehand, however, to make sure you have a commitment from them to help out in an emergency. You can also advertise in your local newspaper or on community bulletin boards for an occasional daytime baby-sitter. You could use such a sitter not only on days when your child is sick, but on those days when your regular caregiver is ill or is on vacation.

If your own efforts at finding backup care fail, call your local child-care referral service; some keep listings of family day-care providers who are willing to care for children who have mild illnesses. Be sure to talk to several of the providers on the list before you need their help so you can find out where the providers are located and how much they charge: You may find that sick care is more expensive than regular care. Your community may also have special centers where children who are sick can receive temporary day care, usually for an hourly fee. To find the names and locations of these centers, check the classified telephone directory. Always visit any sick-care home or center and check its references before you need it to make sure your child will be safe and comfortable there. You must also find out under what conditions they will accept your child.

Warning signs   No matter how careful you are about selecting a caregiver, you may find yourself worrying about the treatment your child is receiving. To ensure that your child is in a safe and nurturing environment, you should be aware of signs that warn she is not. Be alert for indications of physical abuse, such as unusual or unexplained bruises, burns or other marks. Look also for signs of physical neglect, such as a persistent diaper rash. Such occurrences are rare in licensed care, but they have occurred.

Not all abuse is physical, however. Children can suffer mental abuse in day care as well. Look for changes in your child's behavior. Has your happy child suddenly become sullen? Or your quiet child nervous and active? You should also be concerned if your child begins to act listless, withdrawn or fearful at home, or if she seems to cling to you more than in the past. Be watchful, too, for changes in your child's behavior when you part from her in the morning. Does she seem tearful, anxious or frightened? Does she pretend to be sick or hurt to keep you from leaving her? Of course, most children express some anxiety or fear about day care during the initial adjustment period, and many later pass through stages when they strongly protest going to day care.

The possibility of sexual abuse in day care has been a subject of growing public concern in recent years *(pages 64-65)*. One of the big issues in such cases is whether young children are always telling the truth when they report such behavior. Certainly young children can fabricate wild stories, but they are not likely to be able to make up stories in domains in which there has not been some sort of real experience. If your child ever tells you about any suspicious events that might be occurring in her child-care setting, you should immediately investigate.

Your reunion with your child can also alert you to problems. A child who is often hungry or wet when you pick her up, or who does not greet you enthusiastically, should raise your concern. The same is true if your child is too eager to leave in the afternoon. Most children like to dawdle when their parents come to pick them up, or they want to have show and tell about some of the day's events. If your child is frequently standing at the door or gate anxiously looking for you, you should find out why.

Sometimes, parents worry that their child's caregiver has simply become indifferent toward her charges. A parent may suspect that either his child or the caregiver is watching TV all day and doing little else, or that the caregiver is spending most of her time on the phone or doing housework, rather than engaging the child in play. You might detect a tone of indifference through your conversations with her. Does she talk in detail about your child's day or give you broad generalities? Do you always get a rosy report about your child's behavior and activities during the day, or do you get a more realistic account that indicates the caregiver spent time working or playing with your child?

When to take action If you ever believe a particular day-care arrangement is threatening your child's physical or mental health, take him out of the arrangement immediately. Physical or sexual abuse should be reported to the office of child welfare and the agency responsible for licensing child care in your area. Other concerns about health and safety at a day-care home or center, such as unsupervised children or unsanitary conditions, should also be reported.

Usually, however, a parent's doubts and concerns about a particular day-care arrangement involve more benign issues, such as a worry that the child is not getting enough attention or is not spending enough time outside. You may wish to try resolving these issues before seeking another arrangement.

Before confronting your caregiver, however, consider whether your criticisms of her stem more from your own feelings of guilt than from anything she may or may not have done. You may be finding fault simply because you worry about not being home to care for your child yourself. Is the matter you are upset about really important to your child's well-being? Is it something you can reasonably expect your caregiver to do? For example, expecting your family day-care provider to conduct long and involved projects with your child every day when she has five other children to watch may be expecting too much.

Resolving conflicts If you think you have a legitimate complaint, your first step should be to have a calm, friendly talk with your caregiver about the matter. Bring it up at your next scheduled meeting, or if that seems too long a time to wait, ask to meet at an earlier date. During the meeting, be matter-of-fact rather than accusatory. If you have been pleased with most aspects of the care your child has received, then tell your caregiver that first. Be explicit about your concerns, however. Tell her exactly what is troubling you and how you would like to see the problem resolved. Give reasons for your concern.

After you have met with your caregiver to voice your concern, wait a week or so to see whether she makes the change you requested. With some issues — such as asking a caregiver to give

An Expert's View

Protecting Your Child from Sexual Assault

We all know about the sexual abuse of young children. What many of us do not realize is that there are several preventive measures every parent can take to guard a child from such trauma.

Molestation can occur almost anywhere — in school, in day-care centers and even at home. Although there is no clear profile of a molester, no easy way to determine if a given individual poses a threat, concerned parents should screen child-care centers, baby-sitters and other caregivers to reduce the chances that their children will become the victims of sexual offenders.

Certainly a child-care center should be carefully selected. Ask for references on all staff members, and that means janitors and aides, as well as teachers and administrators. When you receive the references, check them out.

Visit the center with your child and look it over thoroughly. Make certain that there are no places off-limits to you; if there are, find out why.

Tell those in charge that you have talked to your child about sexual assault. Ask them whether they ever discuss the problem with the children.

Watch the members of the staff interact with their charges. How attentive and observant are they? How do they respond to a youngster who is hurt or who misbehaves? Make sure that you agree with the methods of discipline at the child-care center.

Get in touch with other parents who have children at the center and find out what they think of it and what their children have to say about it.

Once you have decided on a center, try it out for a set period. Know your child's proposed schedule and who is with the child at naptime or when he goes to the bathroom. Occasionally visit the center unannounced.

Finally, if you have doubts about the center, or if you suspect that your child has been mistreated there — even if there is no evidence of sexual assault — do not hesitate to report your reactions to the state agency responsible for licensing centers or for investigating child abuse. Merely withdrawing your child without saying something about your suspicions means that the children still at the center may be at risk.

When it comes to choosing a baby-sitter or other caregiver, again ask for references and check them out. All molesters are not adults: Some are teenagers. Finding a baby-sitter through friends or neighbors gives you a chance to learn something about the young person you are considering using. While there may be no clear profile of a molester, adolescent offenders often turn out to be loners who are picked on by other teenagers and who are experiencing difficulties in school. Many of them were themselves victims of sexual assault. After a sitter or caregiver has been at your home, follow up by asking your child how it went.

In most reported cases, sexual abuse of children is committed by males, but some 20 percent of the male victims and 5 percent of the female victims are molested by women. And perhaps as often as 90 percent of the time, the victim knows the abuser. In fact, the statistics reveal that in more than 60 percent of the cases, the perpetrator is a member of the victim's own family or a family friend.

A great deal of sexual abuse of children could be prevented if mothers and fathers were to forewarn their youngsters. Understandably, many parents find talking to their children about the problem difficult. They do not want to frighten their children or instill in them unhealthy sexual attitudes. But experience has shown that there are indeed things that you can say and do that will make your child aware of the problem without having a negative effect on him. Teaching children how to protect themselves from sexual assault is as important and as natural as expecting them to obey rules concerning their health and safety.

Educating preschool children about sexual assault requires a different approach from that taken with older children. Preschoolers do not reason abstractly; concepts of acceptable or unacceptable sexual behavior are beyond their understanding. Distinguishing a good touch from a bad touch is difficult for them, unless the touch happens to hurt. The preventive education of preschool children thus must be very specific. It is a good idea to be able to refer to body parts by name.

You can begin by telling your child the following:
- Your body belongs to you. No one — not even a family member — may touch you in ways that make you feel uncomfortable, particularly if the areas touched are ones we normally consider private and cover with our clothes.
- If this ever happens to you, you should tell me, another parent, your teacher or some other adult you trust.

With young children, the message should be repeated often but gently. Some parents find that it can be reinforced by playing the "what if" game: "What would you do if anybody started to touch you and it felt uncomfortable?" Here is a chance to help the child shape a ready answer: "No, don't touch me." Other parents have found that the "say no" game also works. Here parents and child take turns asking each other to do something bad and then giving no as the answer. Through such play, a child can be taught how to say no convincingly: "No. I don't want to do it."

As awareness of the need to protect young children from sexual assault has grown, several juvenile books have appeared that address the problem sensitively through words and pictures and that manage to convey the message without generating anxiety. You may want to get one of these and read it aloud to your youngster.

Although more developmentally sophisticated than preschoolers, children in kindergarten and the first grade can also be confused by abstract concepts. It is better therefore to speak to them in concrete terms and give them examples of how you would expect them to behave in a potentially harmful situation.

In addition to making your child aware of the problem, you should learn to recognize the signs that indicate sexual assault may have taken place. These signals include urinary infections, genital irritations or unexplained bruises. The child may also be behaving differently — having nightmares or difficulty in sleeping, exhibiting fear of a certain person or place, or showing inappropriate sexual behavior.

You should also listen to what your child may be trying to tell you. It is often hard for a child to speak about the experience. Fear can be a factor: The molester may have even threatened the child with injury or injury to you.

You should be prepared to ask the child questions in a calm and loving manner:

- Did someone touch you in a way that did not feel good?
- Who touched you? Was anyone else there?
- Where were you touched? Where else?
- When did this happen? Did it ever happen before?

Even if the child's answer is faltering or evasive, as long as the child describes an abuse, it is best to believe him. Children rarely lie about such experiences.

An adult hearing a child describe a sexual assault is likely to be horrified by the account and to feel anger toward the perpetrator. Such a reaction is only normal. But a child may misinterpret your anger, taking blame for the assault. Indeed, children often feel guilty about their experience, especially if the molester employed trickery, bribery or threats to ensnare them. Just how terribly ambivalent and complicated a victim's emotions can be is recalled by an adult who was molested as a youngster: "I was really concerned because I was having these sexual feelings, of enjoying it, of being terrified, of being anxious and of being very confused. . . . For a child who does not know such things, it is an added layer to be dealt with. The body responds in certain ways whether you like it or not."

Thus the adult must take pains to relieve the child of any self-imposed blame by stressing that the young victim is not at fault and can in no way be held accountable for what happened. It is equally important for the adult to let the child know how glad she is to have been told about the experience and to express concern for what happened. At such a difficult time, holding or cuddling the child provides much-needed security.

To further allay his feelings of fear and anxiety, the youngster should be protected at once from the suspected offender and the child's story should be reported as suspected abuse immediately to the authorities. The victim should also be examined by a pediatrician, even if there appears to be no injury or other outward sign of molestation. Later, the parents may well want to get psychological counseling for the youngster and themselves. The emotional upset that is the aftermath of a sexual assault is never easy for anyone in the family; talking about what happened helps to reduce the pain.

As a parent, you can hope that your youngster will never become a victim. Remember, however, that when it comes to thwarting sexual abuse, the front line of defense is awareness, supervision and the willingness to discuss molestation frankly and openly with your child. Children who know of the danger and know what to do about it will not be easy prey for molesters.

— Anne H. Cohn, D.P.H.
Executive Director
National Committee for Prevention of Child Abuse

a child more personal attention — the change may be difficult to spot. Your child may be your best indicator. Of course, you could always ask the caregiver how the changes are working out. If things do seem to improve, be sure to tell your caregiver you appreciate the changes she has made.

If after a reasonable waiting period the change you requested has not been made or your child remains unhappy, you may want to make an unannounced visit to the day-care home or center, or to your own home if you have in-home care. Watch how your child interacts with the caregiver and, at a day-care home or center, how he plays with the other children. You may find an important clue to what is troubling him. You may also find reassurance that the situation is not as bad as you thought.

Changing a child-care arrangement

If your dispute with your caregiver is either irreconcilable or nonnegotiable, you will have to terminate the arrangement and find a new one for your child. How you handle the situation will depend on the reason for the termination. Sometimes, an in-home caregiver does something that requires you to dismiss her right away. You may discover that she is drinking on the job, for example, or that she is stealing things from your home. In these cases, you should tell her that you are removing your child from her care immediately and that she can expect no reference from you when she seeks new employment.

More often, a parent ends an arrangement because something makes the parent uncomfortable. The parent may feel that the chemistry is just not right between the family and the caregiver, for example, or that the environment at a particular day-care home or center is too chaotic or too highly structured.

Be as specific as possible when announcing your intent. If it is because your in-home caregiver is chronically late arriving or because she has not been willing to help toilet train your child, then tell her so. Be sure to acknowledge the good things she has done with your child, but explain that your differences with her are so great that you must end the relationship. Tell her she can come to you for a reference for her next job.

When you make the decision to end a particular arrangement, you may want to give the caregiver severance pay or one or two weeks' notice — depending on how long the arrangement has been in effect, your relationship with her and your reasons for the termination. Be sure to check the original written agreement with her to see what you had agreed to do in the event one of you felt it necessary to end the day-care arrangement. If possible, try to find a new day-care situation for your youngster before you let a caregiver go. Otherwise, you may find yourself under a great deal of pressure and may accept another less-than-adequate arrangement.

Sometimes it is the caregiver who chooses to end an arrangement. An in-home caregiver may decide to move away. A family day-care provider may retire after her youngest child graduates from college. A day-care center may suddenly go out of business. Or a caregiver may feel a particular youngster is too difficult for her to handle. Finding new day care under such circumstances can be difficult, especially if your caregiver gives you only short notice of her leaving. But, again, try your best not to make too hasty a choice. If your family day-care home or center is closing down, it may be a good idea to contact other parents who have children there to see whether you can join forces in finding new care. By working together, you may be able to arrange to keep the children together. Going into a new day-care situation with old friends can make the transition easier for your child.

The time may come when you will need to change your child's day-care arrangements. If it does, make sure you offer the youngster extra love and support as she gets used to new children and new caregivers.

Making a change

Changing day care can be upsetting for a child, and his behavior might alter as a result. Whether the caregiver was let go or left for her own reasons, your child might feel that he drove the caregiver away because he was bad. A parent must help her child express his feelings and then reassure him that his being naughty was not the reason for the change. Another child might become more aggressive because of anger over the loss of that special person. If this is the case, parents must continue to enforce the limits of behavior the child is used to and not grow overly lenient in an attempt to compensate the child for his loss. During this time, the child needs the security that consistent, loving parents provide. In addition, if it is possible, some type of communication with the former caregiver — through visits, letters with pictures enclosed, or phone calls — will help the child understand that the caregiver did not abandon him.

If your child must leave a familiar group and he seems sad about not seeing his old friends again, reassure him by suggesting he invite those children to your home on weekends. If he seems anxious about the new setting, offer to take him there for a preliminary visit. There may be a few tears and a few fears as your child makes the readjustment, but with your patience and sensitivity to his needs, he should soon be as comfortable in the new situation as he was before. ∴

Balancing Work and Home

When a working mother and her four-year-old daughter — both with brief cases at hand — bid farewell to each other in the morning, it may be the child who sets off for day care with ease and confidence: The child's mother may still be unsure about the arrangement. Although finding good child care can alleviate many of the worries of a working parent, it cannot eliminate all the stresses that come from trying to balance the often conflicting demands of career and children. Juggling family and work is a difficult and delicate undertaking, and despite your best efforts, all the balls can come tumbling down at any time. Only minutes from a meeting at which you are scheduled to give a presentation, your day-care provider calls and informs you that your daughter has a high fever and should see a doctor right away. Or on the afternoon you had promised your son you would come home early to bake cookies with him, your boss asks you to stay late to finish an important project.

Sometimes the conflicts become so numerous and stressful for a working couple that one parent — most often, the mother — decides to put aside professional ambitions and care for their child full time. This can lead to even more stress, however, as the family struggles to get by on one income or as the parent who interrupts a promising career becomes resentful.

Fortunately, dropping out of the work force is not the only option. Some parents switch to careers that give them more time and energy for their children. Others find new employers who are more accommodating to working parents, or they reshape their jobs to better fit the needs of their families. And some of the pressure you may feel can be relieved by adjusting the pattern of your family life, rather than your working life, to provide more daily joy for both you and your child.

Jobs and the Working Parent

The ideal time to consider whether your job is compatible with raising children is long before you become a parent; that way, you can make whatever career changes you believe necessary well in advance of dealing with the demands of a new baby. Unfortunately, it is sometimes difficult to plan your life so far ahead. But whether you are prudently laying the groundwork for parenthood in the remote future or are confronting the immediate reality of a child on the way or already here, avoid making any hasty career decisions based on vague feelings or on guesswork. Approach the issue analytically.

Evaluating your job

A self-employed mother works at home (below) while a paid caregiver looks after her child (opposite). Parents working at home often employ child-care help but are handy if their children truly need them.

Start with a careful assessment of your present job in terms of its effects, or likely effects, on your performance as a parent. Ask yourself the following questions:

Do you have some freedom in determining your working schedule? Generally, the jobs most suitable to raising children are those that give you the greatest control over when and where you work. Self-employed people such as accountants and attorneys in private practice, freelance writers and graphic designers, piano teachers and tutors usually enjoy the most control. But some company jobs may also have relatively flexible hours. Among these possibilities are real estate agent, cab driver and sales representative.

Is your job physically or mentally exhausting, or can you leave it at the end of the day with a good portion of your energy intact? Raising a child requires a great deal of energy; if you use up that energy at work, you will have little left for your child. And the more stressful your job, the more likely that your home life, too, will be stressful.

Does your job require long hours of overtime or overnight travel, or can you finish your assignments within a fairly standard workday? Obviously, jobs that often require you to stay late or to work weekends or that involve frequent travel will conflict drastically with your role as a parent. Some fields notable for such problems are journalism, public relations and restaurant management, as well as any field that involves responding to emergencies, from plumbing to medicine to police service.

If you decide that your present job is incompatible with raising children, you may want to consider changing to a whole new career, one that will give you the time and flexibility you need. However, if such a switch is impossible or would cause too much disruption in your life, you may wish to try changing employers instead. (A cautionary note: In most cases, it is unwise to take on a brand new job while you are still getting adjusted to life with a brand new baby.) Look for a new employer whose benefits, policies and attitudes reflect an understanding of the problems of working parents — a company, for example, that is generous with maternity or paternity leave, or offers day care for its employees' children on the premises or nearby, or has a policy of giving a parent time off if a child is ill.

You may fear that asking questions about parental benefits such as these might jeopardize your chances of getting the job. If so, ask whether you can get a written summary of all benefits. If this is not available, and if the interviewer does not mention parental benefits as she orally outlines the company's benefits policies, go ahead and ask. You need the information in order to make your decision. And you might be surprised at the respect you will gain by stating that your family is a high priority.

Federal law prohibits a potential employer from inquiring about your plans for having children: Should an interviewer raise the question anyway, and if you want to avoid making a fuss, you can reply simply that you have no such plans at the moment. Or you might answer with a question: Would having a child affect the job? When the interviewer explains why she is concerned — because the position involves travel — you can address the issue directly, either by saying that it makes the job impossible for you or by explaining why it poses no problems in your case.

Another feature to look for in a prospective employer is the system of adjustable working schedules known as flextime. Employees at some companies, for example, can start work at any time between 7:30 a.m. and 10:00 a.m., as long as they put in an eight-hour day once they arrive. A parent can plan her workday around the opening and closing of her child's day-care center and readjust it on a day when she needs to take the youngster to, say, a doctor's appointment. Some companies allow employees to work a 40-hour week in less than five full days. Be aware, however, that it can be difficult to arrange day care around a 10-hour workday. And such long hours can exhaust a parent and aggravate, rather than alleviate, conflicts between home and job. Federal agencies have flextime for employees who want it, and civil-service jobs tend not to require too much overtime.

Working for yourself
When searching for a new employer, do not overlook the one who would have your family's interests most at heart — you. You may have skills that can become the foundation of a business of your own. A teacher, for example, can start a tutoring service; a secretary can run a typing service; a chef, a catering business. And many professional people — from psychologists to commercial artists — leave staff jobs to become self-employed.

If self-employed, you may be able to work in your own home. In that case, you could try fitting your work schedule to your child's routine, working, for example, when he is sleeping or is playing quietly. Most parents discover, however, that these quiet moments can be infrequent and irregular. Many self-employed people who work at home employ a caregiver for at least part of the day. Meetings with clients, the pressures of deadlines or simply the need for long stretches of uninterrupted work time can make supplementary care indispensable.

Of course, being self-employed has disadvantages. It may take some time for you to build a clientele, and your income could be lowered significantly in the meanwhile. You may discover your new boss is more of a taskmaster than you expected; many self-employed people work longer hours than people with regular jobs. Unless you are willing to work at night when your child is asleep, you might find you have less time to spend with your youngster than when you were employed by someone else.

Taking work home
Changing jobs is not the only option to parents who want less conflict between their private and professional lives. Many instead have convinced their employers to let them redesign their jobs to get more flexibility. If all or part of your job could be done at home as well as at the workplace, for instance, you may be able to talk your boss into letting you work at home at least

part of the time. Writing reports, calling clients and other solitary work could be done at home. At one midwestern computer company, programmers and software writers with children are given the option of working full time — and for full pay — at terminals set up in their homes.

Part-time work Even if you keep the same basic job, working part time rather than full time can make your life much less stressful, particularly when your child is very young. Working reduced hours gives you more time to spend with your child while enabling you to stay current in your field in case you decide to return to work full time later.

In the past, part-time jobs were usually temporary, low-paying positions that provided few benefits and little chance of developing a career. Today a new concept known as permanent part-time work is gaining acceptance among employers. People who have to manage a staff have difficulty trying to work part time, but many highly skilled professionals, from attorneys to zoologists, are now working less than 40 hours a week on a permanent basis, although some of them do have reduced benefits.

Still, working part time has its pitfalls. You may find yourself spending more time with household chores and less time with your child. You may also discover that your responsibilities at work have not been reduced in proportion to your hours: You have to do the same amount of work, but in less time — or stay late to complete it. If you are allowed to restructure your job into a part-time one, you may find it easier to work a reduced number of whole days rather than part days. Day care is usually easier to arrange for full days than for half days. And the fewer days you need to go to work, the more money and time you will save on commuting. If you are still nursing your baby, however, you may find working half days better than working full days, because you will miss fewer feedings.

Job sharing An increasingly popular variation of part-time work is the shared job. Although sometimes a job is shared between a husband and a wife — for example, two teachers or two nurses — usually it is shared between two unrelated people who are fairly similar to each other in education, income needs, previous experience and job skills. The partners can divide the job in a variety of ways. One may work mornings, the other may choose afternoons. Or they may alternate days or work half-weeks, changing the guard at midday on Wednesday. Although many jobs could be split in such a way, the fields that appear to offer the greatest opportunities for job sharing at the present time are medicine, education, administration and personnel.

Before you try job sharing, be sure that you and your prospective job partner have the personalities for it. Job sharers must be more cooperative than competitive; they must enjoy working as a team and be able to share praise as well as responsibilities. Choose as your partner someone with whom you can be frank and open. If you suspect a conflict, look for another partner.

Day care in the workplace
A growing number of employers are establishing day-care facilities on their premises or nearby. If you know about how these centers work and how valuable they can be to a company, you and fellow employees might be able to convince your boss to consider the idea. Some centers are run by the companies themselves, and others are leased to day-care center operators. Occasionally, a group of firms — particularly ones that share an office building — will get together to form one nonprofit center. A company may offer the child care free to its employees, or it may charge parents for all or part of the expense.

Child care at the workplace is a blessing for many working parents. No longer does a parent have to ferry his child every morning and evening to day care. Nor does he have to worry about being far away in the event of an emergency. Children also find it reassuring to know that their parents are nearby. A parent can have lunch with his child, or drop by during scheduled work breaks to read a story or to play a game.

On-site child care is also beneficial for an employer. It can greatly relieve problems of tardiness, absenteeism and job turnover. Absenteeism at one company with a largely female staff of trained technicians, for example, fell by 15,000 work hours within 12 months of the opening of a company-run center for almost 300 children. Within two years, the employee turnover rate had fallen by 60 percent. Other companies that have started their own day-care centers have noted additional benefits, such as a decrease in the amount of maternity leave requested by new mothers and an increase in employee morale and productivity. By projecting the image of a company that cares about its employees, a center also can help recruit new workers.

Other help for working parents
Other companies without their own centers subsidize day care. Some give vouchers that an employee can spend at the day-care center of her choosing. Or a company may purchase slots in a specific center at a group discount and then pass on that savings to employees who enroll their children in the center. Often, day-

When You Take a Business Trip

Here are some steps that may help your youngster stay happy — and keep you from feeling so guilty — when your job requires you to travel.

● Before you leave on your trip, make a tape recording of yourself reading some of your child's favorite bedtime stories, and end each story with a special good-night message. Your child can play the tape before going to bed or whenever she is feeling lonely.

● Hang a map near your home telephone. Each time you call home, tell your child where your business has taken you, and have your spouse or babysitter show her the place on the map so the youngster can mark the location with a special sticker.

● Give your child a calendar on which you have outlined the days that you will be gone from home and explain how to mark off each day as it passes. The calendar will be reassuring visual evidence that you are returning.

● Hide presents around the house for each day you will be away. Give your child instructions for finding the presents either on the tape recording of bedtime stories or when you call each day.

● Give your child something of yours — a photograph or a piece of inexpensive jewelry — to hold while you are gone.

care subsidies by employers are offered as part of a flexible benefits package, where employees can select, cafeteria-style, from among a group of benefits. Some companies maintain listings of care providers, including sitters who will fill in for parents working overtime, and sick-child accommodations. Usually, this service is available to employees through the personnel office. To provide help for parents on those days when a child is ill, a few innovative companies reimburse a parent for all or part of the cost of sending a child to a sick-care center. Some employers even send a health-care worker to the child's home to provide care while the parent stays on the job.

Getting started   Of course, persuading a company to provide day-care assistance of any kind can be a difficult undertaking. Before you approach your employer, talk with other employees who have children and find out what services are most needed. Outline several options for your employer to consider and explain in detail how each option could be arranged. Describe what other companies, particularly those in a similar line of business, are doing to meet their employees' day-care needs. And point out how providing day-care services can help the company by decreasing absenteeism and employee turnover and by increasing employee morale.

If a parent travels   Jobs that require overnight travel can be particularly stressful for working parents, especially for a working mother. Some mothers worry so much about their children that their work suffers and the reason for making the trip — landing an account or gathering information for a report — is compromised.

By careful planning and with a helpful spouse, such problems can be alleviated. If you are the chief cook in your home, for example, you may wish to prepare ahead some of your child's favorite meals to be served while you are gone. Leave your spouse written instructions about any unfinished errands that normally fall to you and be sure he is aware of any activities related to your child that you are usually responsible for. Also, be sure your spouse knows your itinerary — where you will be, when you will be there and how you can be reached.

If you are a single parent, you will have to make many more special arrangements (pages 102-103). ❖

The Value of Parental Leave

The time taken off work after the birth or adoption of a baby is a crucial period that gives parents a chance to adjust to their new roles and to start forming their lifelong bonds with their child. A woman can need from six to eight weeks to recover physically from a normal childbirth. And many child-development experts believe a minimum of four months of close interaction throughout the day is required for bonding between mother and baby. Because your leave is so important, you should start preparing for it as soon as you know a child is on the way — especially by making whatever arrangements are necessary with your employer. Then later you can spend your time off enjoying your new baby instead of worrying about your job.

You may be guaranteed a certain amount of paid maternity leave by federal law. According to the 1978 Pregnancy Disability Act, an employer with more than 15 people on the payroll must treat pregnancy as if it were a medical disability. A woman giving birth must get the same amount of paid leave as employees who cannot work because of illness or injury — usually six to eight weeks — and must be guaranteed to get her job back at the same salary. If you extend this time off with accumulated vacation time or unpaid leave, however, your employer is not obliged to take you back. And if your company gives no leave for temporary medical disability, then it is not required to grant it for pregnancy and childbirth. Men are not covered by this law, but nowadays a growing number of new fathers are asking for — and receiving — more leave than the traditional few days of vacation after the birth of a baby. More than a third of major corporations in the United States now offer unpaid paternity leave.

Of course, a new mother may want much more time off work than the law mandates. Many employers allow longer leaves — some paid, some unpaid, and with varying provisions about what job will be waiting upon the employee's return. If your company does not have a parental leave policy or has one that does not meet your needs, you can try to negotiate a leave that suits you. Raise the issue early, so your employer will have time to make the necessary personnel adjustments. Remain calm and rational even if your proposal initially is rejected. Remind the person you are dealing with of your value to the company, but be sympathetic about your employer's needs. Training

Being close with your new baby is the top priority of your maternity leave. Do not get sidetracked into spending too much time on other matters.

Nearing her leave's end, a mother observes her infant with the caregiver in a family-care group. If you introduce your baby to day care over a few weeks, you can be sure before returning to work that the arrangement is a good one.

and paying someone else to do your job while you are gone will be expensive and disruptive. Assure your boss that you will help make the transition as smooth as possible. Try to get a guarantee that you will get your job back at the same salary and seniority. Once you come to an agreement, ask to have it put in writing or offer to put it in writing yourself for your boss's signature.

Financing a leave   If you will not be receiving paychecks for all or part of your leave, begin saving money to help cover your loss of income as soon as you start planning to have a child. Worrying about money can create stresses that may disturb your relationship with your child. Try to see that your parental leave fund contains enough so that you and your spouse can pay not only regular bills, such as mortgage or rent, but a full month of day care as well. That way, you can ease your child into your day-care arrangement before you return to work. ❖

Combining Career and Breast-Feeding

Returning to your job need not put an end to breast-feeding. Many working mothers continue to nurse, some because they regard breast-feeding as a wonderful, intensely intimate way to reconnect with a baby at the end of a long day of separation. Of course, a mother who bottle-feeds can achieve the same intimacy if she focuses her attention on the child, cuddling him and cooing softly, so you should not feel you are depriving your baby if you cannot, or do not want to, combine work and nursing. Formula can be as nutritious as mother's milk. It does not contain breast milk's disease-forestalling antibodies, but by six months a baby starts producing his own.

If you do continue nursing, you may want the daytime caregiver to feed your child bottles of your breast milk during your absence. You can do this by expressing milk, either by hand or with a breast pump, and refrigerating or freezing it for later use. Or you may find this process too time-consuming and prefer that your baby be given formula when you cannot be present for a feeding. You can run into problems with either approach. Some women just cannot manage to express enough milk, for instance, and some find that skipping feedings without expressing halts their milk production. If you start work before your baby is four months old, try to express milk at the time of missed feedings even if your child is happily accepting formula at home. Otherwise, your milk supply may never become fully established.

Breast milk in bottles If your child is to have breast milk in your absence, start building up a reserve supply some weeks before you return to work. Express small amounts of milk after feedings into glass bottles and freeze the bottles. Always date each on a piece of freezer tape: Breast milk can be kept for 24 hours when refrigerated but up to three months if frozen. Although some working mothers prefer the simplicity and convenience of expressing manually, others opt for the speed of a breast pump, powered either by hand or, fastest of all, by electricity. Ask your doctor to recommend a pump that is effective, portable and easy to clean.

Once you are back at work, find a quiet, comfortable place — a conference room that can be locked or a little-used ladies' lounge, say — where you can express milk in private for about half an hour at least twice a day. You may want to tell your supervisor you will eat lunch at your desk to make up for the time. Be sure you empty your breasts completely at each session. Store the milk immediately in a refrigerator or in an insulated cooler. Do not freeze it until you get home; the milk may thaw on the way there and cannot be refrozen. Explain to the caregiver

Working Mothers Who Nurse

66 My six-month-old eats solids twice a day, so he's not entirely dependent on breast milk, and I'm able to pump milk for the one feeding that I would be giving him if I were home at midday. I use a hand pump. Fortunately, the company nurse's office has a room where I'm able to pump in private during my lunch break. I cannot quite imagine doing it where I thought I could be overheard. On several days I've been so busy at work that I wasn't able to find the time to pump, and I was pretty uncomfortable by the end of the day. Luckily, my child was hungry when I got home so I simply fed him as soon as I got there. I'm glad I decided to do this, because I would have hated to give up the closeness I feel to him when I breast-feed. I know that mothers who bottle-feed feel equally close to their babies, but I find breast-feeding so emotionally rewarding that it would have been a real loss to me to have given it up. 99

66 My sitter was very cooperative about my wanting my baby to have breast milk during the day, and that is a key: Your care provider has to be in favor of breast-feeding and willing to do a little extra, thawing the milk and so forth. I found that the battery-powered hand-held pump was the most convenient for me. I didn't have to worry about finding an electrical outlet. And I had no discomfort at all — except for the one day when I couldn't get the pump to work! 99

66 I started working when my baby was six weeks old. I tried to keep breast-feeding him mornings and evenings, but I wasn't producing enough milk because the demand wasn't great enough. I tried a breast pump. I did find one that didn't hurt — most women I've talked to who have used a pump tell me it was painful — but it would take an hour to produce four ounces. Nobody has that kind of time. And I was getting exhausted, which made my milk supply dwindle more. I finally gave up. I think this idea of a superwoman who can continue to breast-feed and raise a baby and return to work with full energy is just not possible. If women could stop expecting that of themselves and let go of the guilt, we would be a lot happier and a lot less tired. 99

66 I didn't use a pump. I hand-expressed my milk while I was at work, froze it and took it to the sitter the next day. I think every mother who wants to work and continue breast-feeding should try it. Breast-feeding was nice for my baby and for me. I kept it up for two and a half years. Of course, in the end I was only doing it twice a day. 99

66 As an army nurse, I didn't have any choice: I had to go back to work after six weeks. But I was lucky. I found good child care only two blocks from the hospital and was able to go over there and nurse at lunchtime. I also pumped twice during the working day. After about three months, my body rhythms settled down to a routine, and I could plan on pumping at certain times. But until then my milk production had been kind of volatile. I sometimes had to stop what I was doing and use a pump because my breasts got full. It was even more of a problem because I worked in the pediatric department. Often, when I heard a baby cry I had a let-down reflex and my milk started flowing. Nursing is a really nice feeling; you and the baby have a special bond. I hated giving it up, but my child started weaning himself to a cup when he was around seven months old, and by nine months we stopped breast-feeding completely. I cried for days. 99

that the container of milk should be thawed gradually in a pan of warm water. It must not be boiled, nor heated in a microwave oven, or the milk may lose some of its nutritional value. Any breast milk left over from a feeding should be discarded.

Dressing for breast-feeding   To avoid embarrassment caused by leaking breasts, line your bra with disposable cotton squares or breast pads, and replace them as soon as they are damp. Plastic breast shields may be worn for short periods — during an important meeting, for example — but should not be relied upon because they may cause breasts to become sore or infected. Keep an extra blouse or sweater at work so you can change if necessary. Bright patterns tend to show leaks less than white or solid colors. ❖

The Demands of a Dual Role

Struggling to meet the many demands of family and career is an undertaking that is complicated at best — and often downright exhausting. The daily schedule of many a working parent rivals that of a busy politician: Beginning with the early morning scramble to get the family dressed and fed, the pace may not slacken through a lunch hour crammed with household errands and an evening struggle to get dinner on the table while attempting to spend loving moments with the children. Simply put, there is too much to do and not enough time to do it all.

Making this schedule work, week in and week out, requires organization, cooperation and discipline. Moreover, making it work while keeping up your spirits and staying in peak form as a nurturing parent demands a clear set of priorities and a realistic outlook about what you can and cannot accomplish when faced with so many conflicting responsibilities.

Coping with housework

Housework can be a major source of stress when you have too many other things to do. It takes time to shop, wash and iron clothes, scrub floors, prepare meals and do the dozens of other daily and weekly jobs that keep a household running smoothly. When those hours are added to the time demands of being a loving and responsible parent, the total may equal or surpass the time requirements of most full-time jobs outside the home. Clearly, any working parent who is performing these many tasks single-handedly is doing the work of more than one person.

Although more and more men are sharing in household responsibilities, most of these duties still fall to women, whether they are working full time or not. According to one study, 86 percent of women who work outside the home also do all, or nearly all, of the household cleaning, laundry and cooking. In addition, they handle more than 70 percent of the grocery shopping. And 55 percent of them do the family bookkeeping as well. All in all, mothers who work full time outside the home may spend 30 additional hours per week just performing household chores.

Sharing the load

Getting the fathers more involved in the workload at home would go a long way toward easing the stress of working women. If you are a working mother who needs more help with the housework, sit down with your husband and talk about the problem. Describe all the domestic tasks that you do every week; perhaps even draw up a list. Many men are blissfully unaware of the extent and variety of the labor that goes into running a house. Discuss ways you could divide the chores more equitably, or, if you both prefer, ways you could afford to hire out some of the labor. If you cannot manage the expense of a cleaning service, you may be able to afford to pay a young person from the neighborhood to wash and buff your kitchen floor once a week or to clean the blinds and wash the windows when they need it.

You may also need to lower your expectations about how the house is run and to change your definition of clean. Perhaps it is not essential that the beds be made each morning or that every meal measure up to gourmet standards. Certainly such standards are not worth achieving if the hidden cost is a parent who is too depressed, irritable or tired to do her best in her other, more vital role of nurturing the children.

How children can help

As they grow older and more capable, children should also be encouraged to take on household responsibilities. Explain to your youngster that the family is a team and that all of its members have to work together to meet team goals. Most young children love the idea of helping, particularly if they are praised for their efforts. Of course, the assignments that you give to a child must be appropriate to his age and ability. A two-year-old, for example, can be assigned the job of keeping the napkin holder filled or helping you unpack the groceries. A four-year-old may be given the daily task of feeding the family pet.

Help your child take responsibility for his own belongings by providing lots of storage space for toys and clothes. All shelves, cabinets and hooks for hanging clothes should be within easy reach. When things do get to be a mess, try to make a game out of putting everything away. With toddlers, simply getting all the toys picked up is usually enough of a challenge. With preschoolers, you may have to work harder to muster enthusiasm. Try timing your youngster for speed as he races to gather all the blocks and puzzle pieces. You can make it easier for your youngster to dress himself by buying clothes that are

Household chores may go more slowly when the children help, but the payoff is increased time for family sharing. Older children like it best when they can use the same tools that you do.

color coordinated, with all solid-color bottoms and all print tops. Young children can also be shown how to fold and put away their clothes. In order to make it easy for your child to remember where everything goes, you can cut out magazine or catalogue pictures of the various items of clothing — socks, tops, trousers, underwear — and tape them to the appropriate drawers of your child's dresser.

Time management

One of the most important measures you can take to minimize the stress of juggling work and family responsibilities is to organize and manage your time very carefully. At the beginning of each month, sit down with a calendar or day book and mark down all of the events and activities that require your attention. Make the schedule as complete as possible, including activities for the whole family — the child's birthday party, the Saturday afternoon business seminar, the dog's annual trip to the veterinarian. Be sure that you set aside an occasional night for such must-do activities as paying household bills and writing letters to long-distance friends.

If your monthly plan starts to look too crowded, set some priorities and eliminate or postpone less essential activities. By curbing the urge to cram too many activities into a single month, you allow room for those demands on your time that you cannot anticipate — when your youngster suddenly needs extra attention to work through a problem at school, for instance, or when your boss asks you to take on a special overtime project.

Organizing your day

You should also organize your time on a daily level to eliminate excessive stress. If your mornings are particularly chaotic, face the facts and set the alarm for an earlier hour. Analyze the things that most often go wrong in the morning. If the problem is that your child simply hates to get out of bed, wake her a few minutes earlier so she can linger before you really need to have her up and getting dressed.

If she is finicky about her clothes, make it a joint project each night to assemble her outfit for the next day. You may even need to step aside and let her select her own attire. As long as she leaves the house dressed appropriately for the weather and does not have to pose for school photos that day, clashing colors and mismatched patterns will not do any harm. In general, look for anything that you can do the night before, such as setting the breakfast table or packing the lunch boxes. And for smooth getaways, designate a table or bureau by the door as the place where you assemble all the things that have to leave the house with you — including keys, gloves, lunches and trip slips for school or day care.

If dinnertime is your nightly Waterloo, then plan ahead for that struggle, too. Stock your freezer with ready-to-heat meals. The easiest way is to double the ingredients when you cook your favorite recipes, then freeze half for use when you are too tired or short of time to start from scratch. It also helps to maintain a special recipe file with meals you can prepare start-to-finish in less than half an hour.

To keep the children occupied while you fix dinner, have a box of special toys and games that are only used during that time. You may also want to consider hiring a slightly older child from the neighborhood to keep your children entertained during this awkward hour of the day. Even a nine- or 10-year-old can be a big help to you in this role.

The superparent myth

Much of the stress that affects working parents is self-inflicted. Many mothers and fathers today have extremely high and generally unrealistic images of what being a good parent means. They have fallen for the myth of superparent. A supermom is a mother who keeps her family healthy and happy, keeps her house sparkling clean, maintains a busy social life, and remains intellectually curious and physically fit. Supermom does all of this while holding down an exciting and rewarding job. A superdad is a father who matches supermom in all regards: working, coaching, nurturing the kids, all the while doing his share at home and in the community.

Those who embrace this myth seem to do so out of an optimistic belief that they can have it all — can be the best possible parent and homemaker without having to give up the material advantages of a second income. Parents under this spell often expect everything to run smoothly. When it does not — when the housework falls behind or the child throws a temper tantrum — they tend to blame themselves. The result can be frustration, guilt and even anger.

Striving to be a superparent can also lead to a kind of physical and emotional exhaustion that some authorities have dubbed parent burnout. Paradoxically, the parents who are most likely to suffer this fate are those mothers and fathers who are the most dedicated and enthusiastic about their child-rearing roles. Excessive stress can cause a host of physical symptoms — such as headaches, indigestion, rashes and back pain — and it can lead to more serious problems such as ulcers and colitis, as well. Stress can also cause emotional problems, such as depression and apathy, and it starts some parents in the direction of drug abuse and eating disorders.

Avoiding parental stress

Mothers and fathers who truly want the best for their children will take care to avoid this kind of excessive stress. The first step is to acknowledge that nobody is as talented, disciplined and energetic as the glorified mother and father of the super-parent myth. Realize that you cannot do everything and still have time and energy to be the loving, flexible parent you want to be. This is especially true during your child's early years, when the demands of parenting are particularly taxing. You will have to trim back your expectations, both at work and at home. You should avoid taking on too many jobs at once. If you find yourself organizing a charity drive at work, playing Santa Claus at the nursery school and editing a friend's doctoral thesis on top of your responsibilities as husband, father and employee, then you are probably stretching yourself too thin. You must reexamine your priorities and learn to say no when people ask you to take on added commitments.

Teach yourself to recognize your own early signs of stress — a neck ache, problems sleeping, irritability — and take remedial steps at once. Take an afternoon off to sleep or read, perhaps, or call a friend for lunch. Studies have shown that sharing your feelings with close friends or your spouse will help keep you happier and healthier. Exercise is also a great stress reliever. Spend your lunch hour in an exercise class; or at a minimum, you should develop the habit of taking short, brisk walks before or after work.

Guilty feelings

It seems that a good many parents strive to be superparents out of feelings of guilt. The sources of this guilt are as varied as the parents themselves: Some worry about not being able to stay home when their youngster is sick; others feel guilty about commitments at work when they do stay home. Some mothers regret having to wean their babies at an early age; others fret about the time spent with their careers on hold while they stay home to nurse and to nurture. Most parents find some occasion for guilt in the countless little details of lives stretched thin between family and career. It may be feeding their child peanut-butter sandwiches three days in a row, not signing her up

Children are apt to feel left out when you talk on the phone. Ask your friends not to call at awkward times — such as when you first get home from work. You can also screen your calls with an answering machine.

for dancing or karate lessons, neglecting to buy the present for a playmate's birthday party or forgetting the party altogether.

If you constantly feel the strain of such guilt, it can lessen your effectiveness as a parent. Guilt tends to hamper your ability to follow your best instincts in decisions about day-to-day care. It may, for example, encourage you to give in too easily to your child's every whim and request — with the result being a spoiled, overindulged child. Guilt can also affect your career by distracting you from your job and from possible opportunities for advancement.

Surveys of parental attitudes have revealed that mothers and fathers who work out of financial necessity are less likely to feel guilty than parents who work simply because they enjoy their jobs. Fathers also experience fewer pangs of guilt than mothers — probably because many women are still struggling with uncertainty over the traditional view that mothers should be home with their children.

Dealing with guilt You can take a giant step toward ridding yourself of guilty feelings by realizing that most of the worry is groundless. Your youngster will not suffer irreparable harm if you happen to buy a Halloween costume rather than make one for him by hand, or if you let him watch cartoons on a Saturday morning while you get a little more sleep. In addition, you should try to keep sight of the good things that your work outside the home brings to your family life — a more satisfied and fulfilled parent, for example, and a higher standard of living. Be realistic about what life would be like both for you and your child if you did stay home with him rather than pursue your career. Would your youngster really be better off?

In instances where you feel that your guilt is justified, take prompt steps to change the situation. If you find yourself constantly telling your four-year-old that you are too busy to play with him, for example, then you ought to sit down and figure out a way to make more time in the evenings. Perhaps you can delay dinner by half an hour or leave the kitchen cleanup until after the youngster has gone to bed. If you are uneasy about your choice of a day-care center, then you should make it your priority to find a more workable alternative. Sometimes, just making a list of all the things that make you feel guilty will help you see more clearly where changes need to be made and where you should simply learn to be more accepting. Remember, it is always easier for a child to be happy with his parents when his parents are happy with themselves. ⁘

Shared Family Time

The hours after everyone gets home at the end of the day may not seem to offer great hopes for loving moments together. After all, there is dinner to get together, then chores to be done, baths to be taken, heads to be shampooed — and all before bedtime, which comes quite early for little ones. Nevertheless, if your child is going to remember the fun of family life rather than the stress of a too-busy schedule, it will be because you make a special effort every day of the week. Even if you have to mix some of the playing, listening and loving with the cooking, bathing and tucking-in, you must somehow find time to share. With small children, you cannot save all the loving for weekends.

What is "quality time"? Some beleaguered working parents lean far too heavily on the conscience-soothing notion of quality time: the idea that they can make everything all right — the long days apart, the over-wrought mornings and evenings — just by setting aside a few special moments each day or by planning a big treat on Sunday. Obviously, such a feat is unlikely.

Many child-development experts suggest that parents regard quality time in a broader light and think of it as any shared moments when they are focusing their full attention on their youngster and her concerns, whether in face-to-face communication or an activity they are pursuing together. Children very much need this kind of time; they need to sense that what pleases or bothers them is just as important to their parents.

Your special shared times can be as long as an all-day outing or as short as the time it takes to reassure your toddler when she falls down. The quality of your interactions comes not from their length, but from the complete attention that you give to your child. If you spend two hours playing a game but are preoccupied with deadlines at work all the while, she is likely to sense your detachment, and the time may not turn out to be as meaningful or satisfying to her as you had hoped.

The importance of undivided attention By sharing special times with your child, you are sending your little one several important messages: "I love you," "I enjoy being with you," "You are important to me." These messages build confidence, boost self-esteem and deepen the loving bonds between you and your youngster.

Despite these benefits, unfortunately, parents spend a surprisingly small amount of time, on average, interacting directly with their children. In one study, mothers employed outside the home were found to spend an average of only 11 minutes each weekday and 30 minutes per day on weekends giving their children undivided attention while reading, talking or playing with them.

Mothers who stayed at home full time devoted more time to these activities — an average of 30 minutes each weekday and 36 minutes each weekend day. But experts believe these differences reflect the fact that the children of full-time homemakers are generally younger and thus require more attention. Fathers, the majority of whom worked outside the home, spent even less time with their children — about eight minutes on weekdays and 14 minutes on Saturdays and Sundays.

Making the time   To a certain extent, your special family times have to be created out of everyday events. The time spent bathing, diapering, feeding or clothing your infant, for example, is used to best advantage if, instead of just performing these activities by rote, you focus on your baby and talk to him or play with him. The time it takes to drive your children to and from the day-care center can also be a time for sharing; try singing songs together, telling stories or conversing about the day's events.

Other chances to let your child know he is important tend to spring up unexpectedly. When he scrapes his knee and comes to you for a hug and a bandage, for example, take the time to be

An Expert's View

New Models for Family Life

In a household where both parents work outside the home, there is often a great deal of worry about the quantity and quality of time available to spend with the children. Part of the problem, I believe, stems from the fact that many parents derive their notions about proper family life by recalling images — "playing the memory tapes" — of life in the homes they grew up in. They feel somehow bound to set up the same experiences for their own children, even though in many ways these nostalgic models of family life do not fit their current situations.

I would suggest to these parents that they adapt their ideas about family life to the modern lifestyle, a rethinking process I call "changing the tapes." Many of the tapes that need updating seem to be kitchen memories that cluster around the mother's elaborate food preparations. For example, parents often tell me: "I wish I could be home every day at three to make my children cookies," or "I wish I could make a Thanksgiving turkey dinner the way my mother used to make it."

But your children do not share your childhood memories, and they are open to new traditions. You can develop new ways to share time with your youngsters that will eventually be remembered by them with the same fondness you may feel for your own past.

For example, consider the time when you first get home from work. This is one of the most important times to spend with your children because they look forward to sharing stored-up events of their day. Yet what often happens instead? Mother rushes in and says, "I can't talk now, I have to make dinner," the children respond by whining or crying, and the situation all too easily escalates into an unpleasant and frustrating evening.

Such scenarios often occur when a mother feels the need to re-create the dinner her own mother would have made, with its time-consuming preparations. But today's working mother is not really shortchanging her family if she occasionally serves them a nutritious dinner taken out of the freezer and popped into the microwave oven. On the contrary, cutting down on dinner preparation allows you

more time to give your youngster attention. Why not sit down, have a cup of tea to unwind, offer your little one a glass of juice and relax for a while? On such occasions, dinner can wait. The juice hour before the evening meal may very well become a tape your child plays back with pleasure when he is older.

Like our childhood kitchen memories, many of the time-saving traditions being created by today's parents revolve around dining. The cooperative holiday feast where friends and family bring potluck dishes is one such ritual. Even going out for pizza or a hamburger can become a quality tradition. As a matter of fact, I believe that a whole generation of children will look back warmly on the trip to the fast-food restaurant, because the key to good shared times is not so much the event itself as the spirit involved. You can make any kind of ordinary time special by infusing it with fun and delight in the family's being together.

— Frances Litman
Director, Center for Parenting Studies
Wheelock College, Boston

truly sympathetic about his pain. Perhaps cuddle him on your lap and tell him about a similar accident that happened to you. Minor illnesses, such as colds and the flu, can also provide unanticipated opportunities for getting close to your child. When you stay home from work to nurse a sick youngster, try to look at it as found time rather than an imposition. Spend the days doing whatever he most enjoys: Read to him, play games or just hold him frequently, offering comfort and reassurance.

Special times during the day

Readjustments in your daily schedule can also produce time for the family to spend together. By getting yourself and your children up an hour earlier than usual, you can carve out a special time in the morning for shared activities. Try to get everyone fed and dressed in time to spend half an hour playing a game or reading a book before you have to leave the house. An unhurried start will make the rest of your day seem less hectic, as well.

Whenever possible, reserve the first half hour after returning from work for socializing with your child. Toddlers and preschoolers often need some time to reconnect with their parents. Give the youngster your attention first, rather than opening the mail or turning on the television news. If you have to start dinner right away, invite your child to spend the cooking time with you. If there is room on the kitchen counter, she can sit there and chat. Think of other ways that she can stay involved with what you are doing. Perhaps she can spin the lettuce, mix ingredients or just pass the salt and pepper when you need them. Talk, sing or tell jokes while you work together.

The dinner hour

One of the best and most natural occasions for shared family time is at the dinner table. Sitting down together to eat and talk will reinforce your child's sense of closeness and belonging within the family. Many parents pass up this opportunity by letting the children get in the habit of watching television while they eat. There is nothing wrong with occasionally sharing meals that way, but if you want your family dinners to be events your children will look forward to, let the food and conversation be the main attractions.

Some youngsters are particularly intrigued if you introduce a note of formality, such as candlelight or slightly elaborate table settings. Even very small children can occasionally join you for these events. If your child normally eats earlier than you do, try serving him dessert while you dine.

When your youngster is old enough to talk, encourage him to join in the dinner conversation. Ask him about his day or tell him

Making the Most of Your Hours at Home

As working parents well know, most of the time spent with their children is time borrowed from other responsibilities. In order to give children the attention they need while keeping up with the other demands on your time, you have to be constantly on the lookout for ways to make the most of your nonworking hours. In some cases this means dispatching the chores while your child is asleep or playing at a friend's house. At other times it means finding ways to involve the youngster in what you are doing. Following are several suggestions for using your time more effectively and efficiently:

● Look for opportunities to combine one task with another. For example, set the table for breakfast just after you have cleared the dinner dishes.

● Keep detailed, ongoing lists of the things that you need, then plan your shopping trips with care. The object is to get everything you need in a single trip to the supermarket, department store or home center. Whenever possible, avoid making last-minute shopping excursions.

● Have a family snack as soon as you get home. Make it something nutritious, such as peanut butter, carrots, celery, or cheese and crackers, so that you do not have to worry about spoiling the child's appetite for supper. This will lessen pressure to get dinner on the table. Sitting down with a snack can also be a good time for talking about the youngster's day at school.

● With older children, establish a 15-minute rule that says simply: "I just need 15 minutes to finish what I am doing, then we can talk or do whatever you would like."

● To combine your chores with the child's play, have a place for toys in every room that you use. Choose playthings that are appropriate for each room, so that your youngster will be able to entertain himself by imitating your activities. While you are cooking dinner, for instance, your toddler may want to play with cooking toys. In the laundry room, you could keep clothes-washing toys on a low shelf. And make sure the toys stay in their respective places.

● Invite your youngster to help when you have unusual chores to perform, such as planting vegetable seeds in the garden, chopping kindling for the fireplace or shoveling snow from the sidewalk. Children are more likely to be intrigued by — and enthusiastic about — such seasonal tasks than by more run-of-the-mill household chores.

● Whenever possible, take care of the more time-consuming errands during the week, so that family time can be your priority on weekends. At the same time, reserve for the weekends the kinds of errands that you know your child will enjoy. Some children like going to the hardware store; others enjoy shopping for major family purchases, such as a TV or a new car.

● Make a Sunday morning ritual of reading the newspaper together. Read the comics out loud and summarize for your child the current events.

● Take turns with the children on weekends, so that both parents can have some free time alone to take care of errands and chores.

about your own. Describing your job and the ways that you solve problems at work will help him understand what it is you do and teach him how to talk about his own experiences. Dinnertime can also be used to discuss your youngster's problems and worries, or to reinforce your love and concern for him. Although lively conversations should be encouraged, arguments and personal criticisms should not. Keep this a time of family harmony.

After-dinner games   Although young children love to play games and to work on projects with their parents, surveys show that few families regularly set aside time for such activities. An ideal way to create a regular family playtime is to reserve the hour or so between dinner and bedtime to share with your youngster. Assemble a collection of games, puzzles, kits, workbooks and other projects that can be completed in a relatively short amount of time. If you include games and projects that take longer than one evening to complete, make sure that they can be easily moved to a place where they will be left undisturbed until you are able to resume them. Select activities that are appropriate to your youngster's age and interests, but try to find ones that you enjoy as well. To reinforce the sense that this is a special time for him, let your child select each evening's activity.

Besides giving the family a chance to spend enjoyable time together, games can help a youngster develop new skills and

build on his current abilities. Many games require math, reading or memory skills, which even very young children will gradually absorb as they play. Games also help children develop social skills, such as learning to take turns and accept defeat. Avoid making family games too competitive, however, and do not let them turn into school lessons. The top priority should be having fun while spending time together.

Bathtime and bedtime

Other prime opportunities for giving your child affectionate attention present themselves at bathtime and just before bed. Many children look forward to their baths and will try to prolong them because they know that their parents do not leave them unattended while they are in the tub. If this is the case with your child, allow plenty of time for his bath and enjoy the time together. Let the bath be completely relaxed; perhaps make it a time for silliness and songs.

Young children, in particular, find that a bedtime routine is a reassuring way to make the transition between wakefulness and sleep. Try to plan your evening so that you do not have to rush your youngster to bed. Read a quiet story or talk with him about his day. Some children enjoy hearing a song before they go to sleep or listening to you read nursery rhymes. Some find it comforting to hear the plan for the following day.

If your child acts up at bedtime, it may be a signal that he needs more attention during the day. He may be reluctant to separate from you at night after being apart from you so much of the day. Try not to react with impatience or anger when your child becomes upset or disruptive before bed. Instead, after getting him settled, examine your evening schedule and see if there is any way you can rearrange things to make more time to spend with your little one.

Special events

Apart from seeking ways to make your child feel special in the course of normal day-to-day events, you will want to share activities that are memorable and out of the ordinary. With the exception of special treats such as holiday plays and major sports events, these activities do not have to cost money to be important to your child. For most children, an afternoon at the museum is the height of adventure, as long as they are visiting it with you. A family picnic, well-planned and talked up in advance as great fun, can be just as enjoyable as a meal in a fancy restaurant. Visiting your place of work can also be a special activity. Seeing your office enables the youngster to share a part of your life that may otherwise be difficult for him to comprehend. It gives

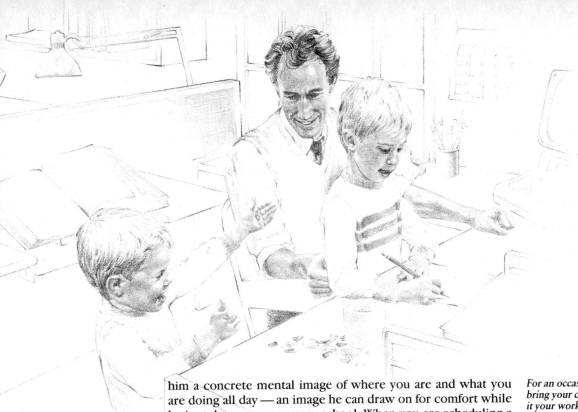

him a concrete mental image of where you are and what you are doing all day — an image he can draw on for comfort while he is at day care or nursery school. When you are scheduling a visit to the office, pick a time that will be least disruptive for your co-workers — at lunchtime, just after the workday ends or perhaps on a weekend.

Some special events, such as the tree-cutting expedition at Christmastime or summer camping trips, become family traditions that are looked forward to with great anticipation. You and your children can have great fun building your own family traditions. You might make every Friday a homemade pizza night and get the entire family involved in the cooking. Or make it a New Year's Day project to sort though the year's crop of family photos and put them in a special album, fully annotated. Whatever events and activities you decide to turn into traditions in your home, make sure that the children are fully involved. They will grow up to remember those times with special affection.

A child's own time Although your child needs special times shared with you, he also needs time to be alone. Take care not to crowd his life with so many activities that he does not have time to develop his own interests and imagination. Follow his lead in this regard. If he is playing quietly and happily in his room, do not feel compelled to rush in and join him. If he sometimes prefers to play with a couple of friends instead of going to the park with you, do not force the issue. Sometimes it is best to wait for the child to request your company. The essential thing is for him to know that you enjoy spending time with him and that you are available when he needs you — or when he simply has something that he wants to share. ∴

For an occasional treat, bring your children in to visit your workplace during off-hours. This will help them understand where you go when you drive away each day and why they cannot be with you.

Baby-Sitters

Whether you have elected to pursue a career or to stay at home with your children, you will undoubtedly need the services of a baby-sitter every now and then. Although an occasional sitter will not spend as much time with your child as a full-time child-care provider does, her responsibilities are just as great during the period when she is in your home. Entrusting your child to someone else's care, even for an hour, is never a step to be taken lightly; therefore, you should apply the same high standards to your choice of baby-sitters that you would use in selecting ongoing day care for your child.

Most parents find that maintaining a list of acceptable and available baby-sitters is a never-ending challenge. At best, baby-sitting is an occupation with a high turnover rate: Teenagers often develop busy social lives, find higher-paying commercial jobs or go away to college; older sitters may move on to other pursuits or other towns. And sooner or later your family may move to a new community, which means you must build another baby-sitter list from scratch.

Much of what is involved in locating, hiring and training reliable sitters is, of course, common sense and parental instinct. This section of the book offers additional suggestions and guidelines, along with ideas about starting a baby-sitting cooperative — a group of parents who sit for each other's children. Used with your own parental know how, the advice on the following pages should help you to relax during your time away from your little one and to return to find a child who is similarly refreshed and in good spirits. As any experienced parent can tell you, leaving a young child comfortably settled with a trustworthy sitter can make the difference between an evening out that is filled with anxiety and guilt, and one that is carefree and enjoyable.

Hiring a Sitter

Any time that you embark on a search for a new baby-sitter, the first step is to consider your particular needs. An active three-year-old may be happiest with an energetic teenager, while an infant is often best left in the hands of an older person who has had experience diapering and feeding small babies and distinguishing fretful gurgles from cries of real distress. Regardless of age or gender, however, anyone who is caring for your youngster should have the fundamental qualities of kindness, patience, sound judgment and a genuine enthusiasm for children. Even an inexperienced person who has these qualities can be trained.

Where to begin your search
The most logical way to begin looking for a person with these attributes is to ask other parents you know to recommend baby-sitters who have done a good job for them. If a survey of friends and acquaintances does not yield good possibilities, you might check notices on community bulletin boards, in neighborhood or church newsletters or in the classified ads of your local paper.

High school and college employment offices, scout troops, 4-H clubs and chapters of the American Red Cross may also be able to direct you to young people experienced at baby-sitting. Student nurses at hospitals are still another resource. If you want a mature sitter, contact senior citizens' groups; some of them are organized specifically to find work for older people.

Baby-sitting agencies offer another option, although it is frequently an expensive one. Be sure the agency you consult screens its applicants carefully for experience and personal qualifications; even so, you should request references.

Checking references
If you are considering hiring a sitter who is trusted and recommended by a neighbor or friend, this may be the only reference you need; the next step is to introduce yourself, explain your needs and arrange a time to meet. On the other hand, when a person's name has come to you by a more indirect route, you should check one or more personal references.

Even though you may be impressed by a prospective baby-sitter's alert, enthusiastic, well-organized manner over the telephone, ask her for the names and phone numbers of two or three parents for whom she has worked. If she has not baby-sat professionally, ask for the name of a person who can recommend her personally; you should also ask about experience she has had caring for children within her own family. It is a good idea to talk with references over the phone rather than accepting letters of recommendation: You can learn a great deal from a person's tone of voice, and some people are more candid in conversation

Interviewing a sitter

than in a formal letter. Find out the age of the reference's children, how long the sitter has worked for the family and what the reference particularly likes about the person.

Arrange to interview a prospective sitter when your child is awake, so you can see how comfortable the two are with each other. At some point, ask the person to do something with your child — hold an infant, perhaps, or roll a ball with a toddler — so you can observe the interaction. Imagine yourself in your child's place and consider how you would feel if left alone with this person. Your basic instincts will help you make a decision.

In explaining the job, be clear about your expectations — for example, do you want a sitter to play with your child or just watch him? Discuss discipline, too, and ask the person what she would do if your child refused to eat his dinner or go to bed. You will probably want a sitter who is a little more lenient than you, since the edge of your discipline is softened by parental love.

And finally, if you are seriously considering hiring a person to sit, the interview is the best time to discuss how much she is to be paid. This amount will depend on her age and experience, the going rate in your neighborhood and how many children you have. Most parents prefer to agree beforehand on an hourly rate, rather than deal with a vague, "Just pay me what you think it is worth," at the end of a long evening. ❖

When you are hiring a new baby-sitter, arrange for her to visit your family a few days prior to her first sitting job. This will give all of you a head start on getting acquainted and will allow the baby-sitter a chance to ask you questions about the care of your children and your home.

Getting Ready to Go Out

An orderly house makes it easier for your baby-sitter to do her job. This does not mean that every magazine has to be neatly tucked away. But it is a good idea to have your child's things in order, first-aid supplies accessible, ingredients assembled for any meal the baby-sitter will be preparing and pets under control. You will also want to talk with your child about the person who will be caring for her and make accommodations for the sitter's own comfort *(box, right)*.

Organizing the household

Getting your home in order before you go out is a matter of putting yourself in the sitter's place for a moment. Try to imagine what it would be like to step into another family's home, play with their child, prepare a meal or bandage a scraped knee. You would need to know where to find any number of things that you locate automatically in your own home.

Chief among these are your child's belongings. You might want to put any clothing she will be wearing during the sitter's stay on a bed or over a chair in her room. If she wears diapers, make sure there are plenty of clean ones in sight by the changing table and that the diaper pail is visible. You may want to gather a few of your youngster's favorite books and toys in one place, too.

Frequently used first-aid supplies, including adhesive strips and an antiseptic, should be assembled in a convenient place, such as a bathroom cabinet. Leave a first-aid manual as well, or written instructions for handling common injuries and minor illnesses *(pages 132-135)*. As a precaution, prepare a medical consent form giving the baby-sitter or another responsible person, who you know will be available, permission to authorize emergency medical treatment. The chances are good that a consent form will never be used, but it would save valuable time if immediate treatment were needed and you could not be reached.

Put a flashlight in a visible spot — on a kitchen counter, perhaps — as a help to the sitter in case of power failure. And a pad of paper and a pencil should be placed next to the telephone so that the baby-sitter can write down messages.

Snacks and meals

Knowing just where to find staples such as peanut butter and bread will make your sitter's job much easier. You might want to collect any food items, cooking equipment and tableware he will need on a shelf or counter.

Before the sitter arrives, prepare precise written instructions about any medicine she must give your child in your absence. To reduce the chance of error, you may even wish to measure out the proper dose in advance, wrap it carefully and set it aside with directions on administering it.

An infant's bottle should be prepared in advance and left in the refrigerator. Provide instructions for heating it and let the sitter know what other liquids the baby may have. A written menu is a good idea when you want your sitter to prepare a meal.

Managing pets

Before your sitter arrives, find out his sentiments about your pet. If there is a problem, such as the sitter's being allergic to cats or uncomfortable with large dogs, it may be wise to confine your pet to one room or the backyard while you are gone. Reassure your child that Boots or Buttons will not be hurt by this experience. If a sitter who is familiar with your home and child agrees to care for the pet, he should be paid an additional amount.

Preparing your child

Your child's reaction to being left with a sitter often depends on how you prepare her for the event. Never fool or surprise a child, hoping she will adjust more easily if you do not give her time to think about your departure. Instead, talk to her casually ahead of time about where you are going, what you will be doing and when you will be back. Although a small child does not have a clear sense of time, she can understand if you explain that you will be there to hug her when she wakes up in the morning.

If you have a baby or an active toddler, you should probably bathe her yourself before you leave for the evening. Not only will this eliminate the possibility of a bathtime accident during your absence, it is a good chance to give your little one exclusive attention before you go. However, when your schedule does not permit a full-scale bath, a quick wash-up — or even skipping the bath altogether — will do no harm for this one night.

Because children feel more secure when they know what to expect, make it clear to your child that playtime, television time, meals and bedtime will be much the same as they are when you are at home. Let her know that the baby-sitter is in charge. Your child will take her cue from you: If you speak confidently about the sitter, your child will learn to approach him with trust. At the same time, allow a child to express any doubts or fears she has about being left in a sitter's care and take them seriously, reassuring her without sweeping aside her concerns.

Discuss with your child, too, what she will do while you are away; you might ask her to choose a special game she wants to play with the sitter or a story she would enjoy having read to her. Holding a special blanket or stuffed animal can offer your child additional security after you have left; if she has such a favored item, you might want to remind her about it before you leave and mention it to the sitter as well. ∴•

When the Sitter Arrives

Even though your child may have met a new sitter, he needs some time to get used to her on the day you are going out. Since you will also want to instruct the sitter and show her around the house, ask her to come 20 minutes to half an hour before you expect to leave, and plan to pay her for this time.

Smoothing the way
You can help your child warm up to the sitter by not pushing him to accept her right away. Instead, let your own greeting set the tone; even a baby will be encouraged by a parent's friendly, trusting manner. Sometimes having the sitter offer your child a new toy or a treat, such as ice cream, helps pave the way to acceptance. But give your youngster a chance to appreciate the sitter for her own merits, too. Let your child listen as you explain such routines as meals and bedtime, appropriate TV programs and suggested activities. At the same time that you are giving essential information, you will be reinforcing the idea that the sitter is in charge and knows how things are to be done.

A tour of the house
Take a few minutes to show a new sitter around your home. Have your child accompany you, and perhaps lead part of the tour. Your youngster's room is a logical place to begin. Point out diapers, clothing, blankets and toys. Mention any special rituals that your child depends on — for example, a story at bedtime.

Remember to point out any relevant idiosyncracies in your home's plumbing and heating systems, such as unusually hot water or odd furnace noises. And as you go through your home, point out items that might be hard for a stranger to find, such as a hidden light switch or a telephone. Other information you will want to give your sitter can be found on pages 100-101.

Before you go, make sure that the baby-sitter is able to operate all safety-related equipment and understands that, should a fire break out, she and the child must leave the house at once and call the fire department from a neighbor's phone.

House rules
The first time a new person sits for you is the right time to discuss any guidelines regarding your child's safekeeping and the sitter's own behavior. The first of these rules, of course, is that she should never leave your child unattended. You should remind her, too, never to open the door to an unfamiliar person, even someone who claims to be a neighbor. A sitter can phone for qualified help if someone at the door is in need of assistance.

Certain house rules apply to a sitter's personal conduct. Consuming alcoholic beverages while baby-sitting is naturally something you will not permit, and if you do not want a sitter to

Say good-by to your children when you leave and tell them when you will be back home. Many children cry at the moment of departure, but the tears are often dry by the time their parents are out of the driveway.

smoke in your home, tell her so. Ask a baby-sitter to limit personal telephone calls to 10 minutes or so, in case you try to call home. You should also clearly state whether or not she is permitted to have a friend visit after your child is in bed. These guidelines may vary from sitter to sitter, depending on the person's age and how well you know her. Spelling out your policies from the start can prevent many problems from occurring. However, even a sitter whom you like and trust may occasionally do something that worries you. When this happens, explain your concerns and make it clear to the sitter that you expect her to change her behavior if she wishes to continue working for you. If you are firm about your disapproval without being harsh, she will most likely try to change.

Saying good-by　　It is wise to let your child — even a baby — see the sitter before you leave. That way if he wakes up during the time you are away, he will not be surprised by an unfamiliar face. On occasions when your child will already be asleep when the sitter arrives, be sure to remind him, as you are putting him to bed, that someone else will be there in your absence.

Many sitters bring along their own grab bag or surprise box containing an assortment of inexpensive toys to engage children once parents have left. Such playthings are more apt to divert a weepy child than his own familiar toys.

Always say good-by when you are going out. Although a child may cry when he realizes you are leaving, sneaking away to spare yourself these tearful displays is not a good solution; such behavior only cultivates a child's mistrust. Saying good-by in a confident, upbeat way will help convey the notion that your child need not fear these brief separations, and he will soon understand that you do, in fact, return each time. Eventually he may discover that having a baby-sitter come in to take care of him offers an interesting and enjoyable change of pace. ⁘

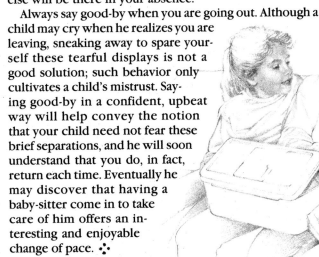

Leaving Clear Instructions

While you cannot expect a new baby-sitter to learn everything about your home and your child all at once, it is important to give clear directions regarding the child's routine, safety precautions and your own expectations for that particular day or evening. Since there can be a great many details for a sitter to remember, take the time to prepare written instructions about meal preparation or any other procedures too complicated to convey verbally.

The check lists on these pages suggest, in addition to day-to-day instructions, the emergency telephone numbers and other basic information that every sitter needs to have readily available — even though many are items she will never have occasion to use. You will probably want to write down your roundup of baby-sitter information legibly and post it on a bulletin board or keep it in a small notebook, and update it as needed. Before you leave a new sitter for the first time, give her a chance to review your written instructions and ask questions about anything that remains unclear.

Whenever possible, you should leave a number where you can be reached in case problems arise. If you are out shopping or otherwise unreachable by phone, you should plan to call home at a prearranged time. And remember to leave a pencil and a pad of paper by the telephone, for the sitter's convenience in writing down messages or in noting any problems or questions she wishes to bring to your attention when you return. ⋄

On Health and Safety

- Instructions on whom to call first in case of an emergency.
- Directions to your home to give to emergency-services providers.
- Any medication your youngster is taking and the proper way for the sitter to administer it.
- Your child's birth date, which may be needed for medical treatment.
- Your child's allergies.
- Potential danger zones inside or outside the house from which your child is restricted, such as a medicine cabinet or a steep staircase.
- The location of first-aid supplies and instructions for their use.
- Exit routes in case of fire.

About Your Child

- Instructions for feeding an infant; appropriate snack foods for an older child; menus for meals that will be served in your absence.
- What is and is not permitted for play.
- Whether your child may visit a friend or invite a friend to the house.
- TV programs your child may watch.
- Activities and books she enjoys.
- Unusual problems or preferences your child may have.
- Ways to comfort your child if she becomes frightened or upset.
- How to handle misbehavior.
- Bedtime and associated rituals; what to do if your child wakes up.

About Your Household

- The location of thermostats and temperature controls, flashlights, any necessary keys.
- How locks on the front and back doors operate.
- How to answer the telephone; how and when the sitter should answer the doorbell.
- How to operate appliances such as the stove, the bottle warmer or the television set.
- Any special equipment or any particular areas of the house that are off-limits to your youngster or to the baby-sitter.
- What the baby-sitter should do if your youngster gets locked in a room accidentally — the bathroom, for example.

A Handy Information Guide

The sample list shown below suggests the items of emergency information every sitter needs to have readily available, including phone numbers to call if she must summon local emergency services, and the names and phone numbers of persons she can contact in case she needs assistance and cannot reach you. Most of the entries on such a form will remain fairly constant; a few will change with each occasion. For convenience, keep your list on a chalkboard or a wipe-clean slate so you can update the information as needed.

Baby-sitter's Directory

Parents' names
Home address
Home phone number
Nearby relative or friend
Pediatrician
Fire department
Police emergency
Poison-control center
Ambulance service
Nearest hospital emergency unit
Taxi company
Medical insurance company
   policy number

We can be reached at this number
We will be home at
We will return at

Special Situations

An infant's first sitter

Rare is the parent who feels no pangs about leaving a newborn in someone else's care for the first time. Do not be concerned if you approach this early milestone in your parenting career with anxiety or even sadness; these reactions are natural and healthy signs of your love and protective instincts toward your child.

Your initial outing after the baby's birth will be less stressful if you plan to be away only a short time and choose a nearby spot — a neighborhood theater or restaurant, perhaps — as your destination. If you are fortunate enough to have the baby's grandparents or other close relatives living nearby, you may feel more comfortable asking them to baby-sit on your first few occasions out.

When relatives are not an option, you will probably want to find a mature sitter who is well experienced in the care of small babies. The extra money you will pay for these services is worth the peace of mind you will gain knowing such a person is in charge back home.

In the beginning, follow your impulses to call home as frequently as you need to. You will soon learn that your child can be safe and happy in your absence, and you will be ranging farther and for lengthier stretches without worrying.

Leaving for longer periods

On certain occasions — including a vacation, business trip or family emergency — you may need to leave your child with a sitter overnight or for several days. In most cases this should not unduly upset a child, but you will want to be sure to leave her with the most trusted, familiar person possible.

Again, grandparents or other relatives are the ideal solution; having them in charge will not only relieve your mind about the quality of care, but it can offer your child the added pleasure of being doted on as well as cared for.

Even if the sitter you choose knows your child and home well, you need to give extra thought to the instructions and telephone numbers you provide. Supply the names and numbers of two physicians rather than just one and designate a responsible adult nearby whom the sitter can consult if she must make a weighty decision and cannot get in touch with you.

A sitter who has cared for your child primarily at night will need more information about the child's daily routines, naptimes, favorite foods and the like. You may wish to suggest a few places for the sitter to visit with your child, but you should also leave room for the two of them to enjoy spontaneous activities.

Before departing, give your child a chance to adjust to the idea that you will be away longer than usual. If you are going on a vacation, for example, you might show her pictures of the hotel where you will be staying. Let her know that you are looking forward to your trip but will miss her. Allow your child to express her feelings, too, about whether she is anxious or excited over this break in the routine.

While you are away, you will want to call in regularly to keep in touch with your child and the sitter — and to reassure yourself that all is well at home.

Taking a sitter on vacation A two-week stay at a beach or a ski lodge can be all the more enjoyable if you have your little one with you but are not constantly caring for him. Taking a sitter along on these occasions can offer you the dual pleasures of your child's company and time to yourself when you want it.

Since the sitter will be spending quite a bit of time with your family, you will want to choose someone you especially like. Before leaving, discuss the sitter's role with her. Will she have some time off during days or evenings to enjoy herself? Do you want her to help prepare meals? Arrange payment that corresponds to her duties and free time, keeping in mind that while you are paying for her room, board and transportation, she will be working hard caring for your child. ❖

Baby-Sitting Cooperatives

Joining a baby-sitting cooperative — a group of parents organized to share sitting services among themselves — provides an economical solution to the problem of finding reliable sitters. Time rather than money is exchanged, and members provide a ready reserve of experienced sitters. What is more, a co-op can be a pleasure as well as a convenience: Parents who unite to help each other in this way often become friends, discovering common interests beyond child rearing.

Getting started

Whether you join an existing co-op or organize one yourself, the first step is to look around your community for other parents of young children. Co-ops are most convenient when the members live relatively near each other, so check close to home first. You might talk with neighbors or parents you see at your local playground, scan the library bulletin board or consult the classified section of your community newspaper. If you are willing to go outside your immediate area, you could ask your pediatrician or perhaps the leader of a local childbirth class about other parents who may be interested in forming a co-op.

Co-ops vary widely in size; some include just a few families, while others stretch to encompass as many as 200. If you are starting a group, a membership of 15 to 20 families is a reasonable goal — one that will provide plenty of sitters without requiring elaborate bookkeeping. You can begin with far fewer, however, and build to your desired membership size. Once you have located at least a few families, you will need to meet to organize the group and establish policies. At your first gathering, draw up a membership list that includes names, addresses, ages of children and times parents are available to sit. You may want to choose officers to run meetings, distribute the membership list and keep financial records, if you charge dues to cover expenses.

Keeping track of hours

The way a co-op keeps track of its members' sitting hours is a major decision that affects the overall operation. There are many variations, but accounting procedures fall into two major categories: One involves keeping an account book of sitting credits or debits; the other consists of exchanging some form of currency, such as tokens or a scrip. In either case, to set your cooperative in motion, you need to advance members a number of sitting hours in the beginning. One reasonable way to calculate this amount is to average the number of hours the various members use sitters each month and credit each family that number of hours or equivalent currency.

If you choose to keep books, your co-op will need to appoint or elect a secretary. Each time a parent baby-sits he calls the secretary, who enters his time and debits the family for whom he has sat. The secretary keeps running tallies of every member's credits or debits. There is usually a limit on how far in debt a family may go before having to return services. Since the secretary knows who is most in need of earning credits, she is often in charge of arranging for co-op members to baby-sit for each other. The secretary's responsibilities can be quite time-consuming; therefore, many organizations rotate the job on a monthly basis and pay the secretary with extra sitting-hour credits.

For small co-ops in which members are in touch with each other frequently, exchanging currency rather than keeping books usually works well. Under this system you will need to print scrip or prepare a batch of tokens — painted pennies or poker chips, for example — to be issued to members in the beginning. The agreed-upon currency is then simply traded back and forth among members, who set up their own sitting times with each other. There is no need to maintain records, unless your co-op wants to have a central accounting system, as well.

Policies and procedures

Your co-op will need to adopt certain policies concerning sitting hours — for example, whether families with two or more children will pay a higher rate than those with only one, whether members will earn more for sitting on holidays and at busy times of the day, and how to figure fractions of hours.

As for sitting procedures, decide how far in advance a member must engage or cancel another member's services. Consider where members will baby-sit; often a parent sitting in the daytime does so at her own home, while nighttime sitting takes place in the home of the family going out. Discuss, too, what kind of preparation and information a sitter should expect. Although parent members may be experienced in the care of young children, they will need to be shown around unfamiliar homes and guided in individual child-care matters.

Keeping the co-op going

Finally, your group needs to consider how it will bring in new members when a founding member leaves or when you want to expand the size of the co-op. You may allow people to enter informally or you may ask, as some co-ops do, that a new family be sponsored by an established member.

A sponsor usually arranges a social gathering at which the new member is introduced. In some co-ops, the sponsor is also held responsible for covering that member's advance of sitting hours if it is not repaid before the new member leaves. ❖

A Baby-Sitter's Guide

This section of the book is designed as a succinct introduction to the art of baby-sitting, included here for parents who wish to leave their sitter a detailed summary of her responsibilities — along with some child-care information to help make her job easier and more fun. You probably will want to read it thoroughly before you give the book to your sitter, so that you will be prepared to answer any questions she might have.

While the material that follows is primarily directed at the level of the young, beginning sitter, it contains information for more experienced hands, as well. The novice should find that the opening discussion of the baby-sitter's role provides a well-rounded orientation to the subject. In addition, the beginner should carefully study the guidelines for basic care found on pages 114-119; these offer practical advice on feeding, diapering and other fundamental chores that make up the job.

The experienced sitter may be more interested in other parts of the guide. She may want to expand her insights into your child's behavior and emotional needs by reading the thumbnail review of child development on pages 110-113. She may also find, among the activities and crafts on pages 122-131, a fund of new ideas that can spark her own inventiveness and make her sitting hours more enjoyable for herself and your child.

Whatever their experience, most sitters should appreciate the final pages — a guide to handling some of the more common illnesses and medical emergencies. And you will feel more comfortable leaving your child with a sitter when she has this information at her fingertips.

The ABCs of Baby-Sitting

Although baby-sitting sometimes is considered a lightweight occupation, in fact it is one of the most serious jobs you will ever have. Your employers entrust to your care the things they love most — their children and their home.

Your role as a baby-sitter is to take the place of the parents while they are away — a job that requires judgment, skill and imagination. You may disagree with some of the house rules, but you should not change them. Above all, remember that children need a stable set of family rules and expectations. So you must park your own beliefs about child rearing at the door and follow the parents' wishes. Here are a few guidelines that should make your job easier:

The preliminaries. When parents offer you a baby-sitting job, ask enough questions to feel comfortable with their requirements. Then explain your usual rates and terms, in order to prevent misunderstandings later on. The discussion need last only a few minutes, but by its end you should be clear on the following points:
- The number of children and their ages. If you feel anxious about taking care of young babies or do not like taking care of several children at once, be sure to say so during the initial conversation.
- What time the job starts. Tell the parents that you would like to arrive about 15 minutes before they leave, so that you have time to learn about the house and the children.
- How long the job will last. If your own parents require you to be home by a certain time, inform your employer.
- How you will get to and from the job.
- Your hourly rate. If sitters in your neighborhood ordinarily get time-and-a-half pay after a certain hour or extra pay for additional children, specify this up front.
- Whether the parents expect you to do housework. While it is reasonable for parents to expect you to clean up after the children, extra housework might prevent you from keeping proper watch over them. Feel free to decline. If you decide, however, that the work can be done — perhaps while the children sleep — you may want to charge extra.
- Finally, make sure that your own parents approve of the terms of the job.

Reporting for duty. By accepting a job, you promise your services to your employer. That promise must be kept even if you later get an invitation for a date or party that you would really rather accept. You should cancel out only if you are sick or if your own parents disapprove of your taking the job. In these cases you should notify your employer as soon as possible, explain your reason, and if possible recommend another reliable baby-sitter.

When you leave for a sitting job, dress neatly but casually, since the work may be messy. And carry a few vital pieces of equipment in your purse or book bag: a pad of paper, a pen, a flashlight, coins for a pay phone and enough money for taxi fare home, if that should become necessary. After you arrive, talk to the parents for a few minutes about the job's details and any potential problems. Write down their instructions and put them beside the phone — do not rely on memory.

Emergency information. Review any instructions the parents have prepared before they leave. You should know the answers to several vital questions:
- How can you reach the parents in an emergency? Write down the places they will be and the phone numbers.
- If you cannot reach the parents, what is the name and phone number of an adult friend you should call?
- Where are phone numbers for the police, fire department, ambulance, poison-control center, family doctor and the nearest hospital emergency room?

The care of the children. What do you need to know about the children in order for the job to go smoothly?
- Do they have special likes and dislikes?
- Have there been any recent problems or special circumstances — such as colic, illness, teething or toilet training?
- How does the child usually behave with baby-sitters? Does she cry or panic when her parents leave? Are there any tricks that calm or reassure her?
- What is the schedule for playtime, meals, snacks, naps, television and bedtime?
- What rules about snacks, TV programs or activities are you expected to enforce?
- What meals should you serve? Know where the food is kept, how to prepare it and what help each child needs.
- Are there special bedtime rituals? Find out each child's habits, from favorite pajamas to night lights, because any little change can upset a child for the entire night. Does a youngster have special nighttime fears or nightmares or does he sleep-walk? How should you handle those situations?

Learning about the house. If the house is unfamiliar to you, here are some things you might want to check out:
- Where are the light switches for each child's room and for key hallways? How do you fasten the sides of the crib?
- How do you control the heating or the air conditioning?
- Where will you find the first-aid kit and supplies of fresh diapers, clothes, towels, sheets, pajamas, bed pads and blankets?
- Where should you put dirty diapers and clothes?
- Are there any pets in the house? If so, ask about their habits, and rules for them. Then get introduced to them. Always approach a strange animal slowly, with your palm up, and let the animal approach you at its own pace.

The baby-sitter's privileges. Find out what behavior the parents expect from you while you are in their home.
- Can you use the telephone? Even if the parents give permission, it is a good idea to keep conversations short. Long phone calls might block incoming calls from the parents or distract you from watching the children.
- Is it all right for you to use the TV, stereo or VCR?
- What can you eat or drink? Thoughtful baby-sitters do not raid the refrigerator without permission.
- Can you have a friend over? Often this is a bad idea, because the friend may distract you from your duties. On the other hand, studying or talking together may help you stay awake at night, after the children are asleep. Even if the parents give permission, do not invite more than one friend. And never entrust a child to your friend's care.

Your key responsibilities. Your first duty as a baby-sitter is simply to watch the child, keeping him happy and safe from injury. Do not let yourself get distracted by TV, homework, visitors or phone calls. Children are quick-escape artists with an amazing capacity to discover or create danger. A good rule of thumb is, do not leave a child to play alone even for a moment, unless he is safely confined in a crib or playpen. An exception may be made for a kindergartner, who can be allowed to play on his own if you look in on him every 10 minutes or so. When a child is asleep, check on him about every half hour.

The second part of a sitter's job is caring for the child, just as his parents ordinarily would. This involves more than only the basics of feeding, changing diapers and putting the child to bed *(pages 114-121)*. You also must be a playmate and an entertainer: Play games, read stories and try some of the activities described on pages 122-131. Be sure to tailor the activity to the child's mood and to the time of day. If the child is full of energy, you might play outdoors; at bedtime or when he is tired or cranky, you should choose a quiet story or song.

Your third job is to be a role model for the child, who will look up to you — and probably will report about you to his parents the next morning. No matter what the parents allow, do not drink alcoholic beverages, use drugs or smoke while baby-sitting. Do not swear or use foul language. And do not snoop through the parents' belongings.

Using good safety sense. Another important part of a baby-sitter's job is to safeguard the house and children — mostly by using common sense and a bit of prudence. When the parents leave, lock all outside doors. Do not open them for anyone unless the visitor is known to you or the parents have told you to expect the caller. If a postman or a deliveryman calls, you should handle the transaction through a closed or chained door. If a stranger wants admission for any reason — to summon help after a traffic accident, perhaps — offer to make the phone calls yourself but do not open the door.

When strangers telephone, ask for their name, phone number and any message, and say that you will relay the message. Do not give out unnecessary information, such as the fact that you are a baby-sitter or the hour the parents plan to return. If you receive an obscene or annoying call, hang up immediately.

If you see or hear anything else that might be a threat to the household — a prowler, perhaps — do not wait for proof. Call the police emergency number at once and stay in the house until the police arrive. And if you encounter any situation that baffles or troubles you — from a baby who will not stop crying to an electrical power black-out — you should not try to struggle through the problem alone. Call for help from your own parents or a trusted neighbor.

Finishing the job. Wash any used dishes and pick up any toys, games or clothing, leaving the house at least as neat as you found it. When the parents return, give them a brief report on what happened in their absence, including any problems that you encountered. It is customary for one of the parents to walk or drive you home. But if an employer appears to be intoxicated or behaves in any other way that makes you uncomfortable, politely decline the offer and telephone your own parents or a taxi instead. •:•

Different Ages, Different Stages

A baby-sitter cannot be a child psychologist, of course, but you will find that a basic understanding of how children think, feel and behave at different ages and stages will help you adapt your baby-sitting strategies to the particular little person you are caring for at the moment. A 15-month-old toddler is likely to accept your help gladly as you zip up his coat, for example. But the same child a year later, stubbornly striving to be independent, may refuse all help and loudly insist on doing it himself. Gaining some insights of this sort into the mysteries of child development will help you avoid problems and can make baby-sitting a happier, more interesting job for you.

In addition to behavior that comes with the child's age, each youngster has his own distinct set of personality traits, virtually from birth, that help to shape the way he reacts to life around him. One child may be rowdy and fearless and given to roughhousing; another youngster the same age may be quiet and cautious and prefer to play with puzzles or read books. You might notice that even children within the same family often have very different personalities.

Still, despite their individual natures, all children go through roughly the same stages of development. And they have the same deep need for your attention, affection and approval at every step along the way. The thumbnail sketches that follow will give you a brief behavior profile of babies and young children as they grow from infancy to the age of six.

Birth to Six Months

For the first few months, an infant is physically helpless and completely dependent on others for his care. He is very near-sighted and can see things best when they are held about 12 to 18 inches from his eyes. His immature digestive system can handle only mother's milk or infant formula, and he must be burped regularly during feedings. His body is very sensitive to slight temperature changes; he must be warmly dressed even indoors and checked occasionally to ensure that he is not overheated or chilled. To make up for such limitations, nature equips each baby with a loud, piercing cry — a built-in distress signal that summons you to take care of his needs.

Although a young baby's life may seem limited to eating, sleeping, crying and filling his diapers, he also is an alert, sociable creature. He thrives on attention; he responds by gurgling, smiling and thrashing his arms and legs about. He delights in being touched and cuddled, in eye contact, in looking at human faces. He likes listening to friendly human voices and to

quiet music; you should avoid sudden noises and loud music, though, because babies have sensitive ears. A young infant also likes to grasp things and feel their textures. For instance, he may grab your glittering necklace or earring — one of the occupational hazards of baby-sitting.

Six to 12 Months

As a baby grows, she quickly becomes more active and mobile: At six months she often can sit by herself, and soon she can crawl almost anywhere. The baby also develops enough skill with hands and fingers to grab things, play with food, push away bottles and put nearly anything into her mouth. She must be constantly watched whenever she is outside her crib or playpen, so that she does not get herself into position to roll off a bed, tumble down stairs, pull something down on her head or stick a toy — or her finger — into an electrical outlet.

Although the baby probably still nurses or bottle-feeds part of the time, she can also sit in a high chair now and eat soft foods. Since the child is too young to learn table manners yet, at

Babies love to be held, smiled at and talked to — even though they cannot understand the words you are saying. Hold a young baby securely and confidently; if you handle him gingerly or jerkily, your motions may make him anxious and fussy. And you should be sure to cradle a young baby's head, because his muscles are not yet strong enough for him to hold it up on his own.

mealtimes you must accept the inevitable mess. A bib helps, but usually you will end up wiping off both the child and the furniture after each meal.

The baby's interest in the world increases a lot during these months. She begins to understand the meaning of names and words; she imitates sounds and waves good-by. She has a vague understanding of the word "no," but you should reserve it for critical situations. She still loves to be held, but now she also takes a greater interest in toys. Her attention span is slightly longer, and she enjoys repetitive games such as pat-a-cake. When bored, she will whine or cry to get your attention.

During this period, the baby grows more deeply attached to her parents. She learns to tell the difference between familiar and unfamiliar faces, and she may act shy, anxious or alarmed around strangers — particularly those who come on too strong at first. Because the baby has no realistic sense of time, she may feel that every separation from her parents is permanent and may cry when she sees them go. To ease such problems, try to spend 10 or 20 minutes with the family before the parents leave, so the baby can get used to you. If she fusses later, your patience and understanding will help calm her down.

Excited by their new ability to get around, curious toddlers can create havoc anywhere in an instant. When baby-sitting for children this age, you need to keep a wary eye on them — leaving them free to play and explore, but quickly stepping in when their explorations lead them into drawers and cabinets.

12 to 18 Months

During these months, the baby rapidly becomes a young toddler, learning to climb, walk and run. His hands are nimble and busy, transforming him into a tireless explorer whose curiosity can lead to mischief. Not only can he hold a drinking cup and spoon and scribble with a crayon, he is becoming quite a little wizard at opening cabinets and drawers. Parents and baby-sitters alike need to strike the right balance between freedom and overprotectiveness. You must allow the child room to investigate, struggle and make mistakes, so that he can learn to master his world. But you must watch closely enough that you will be ready to intervene before he hurts himself, damages something or becomes extremely frustrated.

Such guidance is complicated by the toddler's limited reasoning abilities. A child this age is incapable of foreseeing potential disasters: The whole notion of rules is still a mystery. And because he has a short memory, he cannot learn very well from scoldings or experience. So rather than explaining problems, you must solve them directly — by removing hazards and distracting the toddler from no-win situations.

A toddler is generally fascinated by language and is beginning to build a small vocabulary. He loves to listen to his own voice,

often repeating the same two or three words over and over. If you name objects around you or pictures in a book, he can point to them. And he can follow simple verbal instructions.

During this period, you may find that a child's moods are very changeable. One moment he may be playing contentedly alone, then abruptly demand to be cuddled like a baby. Try to take this seesawing in stride; he is balancing the exciting new skills he is learning and the scary feelings that come with his newfound independence.

18 Months to Two Years

As the toddler nears the age of two, she steadily becomes more active. She walks and climbs confidently and begins to learn to dress and undress herself — often a time-consuming process. Ask the parents which steps in her bedtime routine she can handle alone and which ones need your assistance. Then tactfully offer whatever help is required.

The child at this age is intrigued by other children. She likes to play beside them at playgrounds and parties, but she is still too self-absorbed to interact with other toddlers. She cannot yet grasp the "do unto others" principle of give and take: She may unthinkingly grab another child's toys or shove a playmate aside, yet she will protest bitterly if she is treated this way.

The toddler cannot yet understand potential dangers or analyze complicated problems. But she is increasingly opinionated and self-assertive. She may become jealous when siblings get your attention. She learns about ownership of objects and proudly shows off her possessions, proclaiming them, "Mine!" And at this age, she is easily frustrated. Because she does not fully understand rules or social conventions, she may express this frustration or anger by throwing temper tantrums. Mild ones you can ignore, but you should be ready to step in if the youngster reaches the point where she may hurt someone or break something *(page 119)*.

Two to Three Years

During this busy year, the toddler matures from a walking baby to a relatively self-sufficient child — a difficult transition period often nicknamed the "terrible twos." True, his stepped-up efforts to be his own person and make his own way in the world can lead to some pretty stubborn behavior. But in his good moments — and there are lots of them, really — the two-year-old is charming. He is less impulsive than younger babies and now is beginning to follow simple rules. He likes to imitate adults and will happily help with housework and errands. And he can be quite affectionate toward those around him.

As he learns to assert his own power and independence, the two-year-old becomes fascinated by decisions. He is often bossy and demanding, yet indecisive at the same time: If you suggest wearing white shoes he will insist on blue ones, but after you have fastened those on he may demand white ones after all. He says "no" often — but mainly to experiment with a powerful word that seems to give him some control.

You can avoid such exasperating negative behavior with a little foresight. Instead of asking questions that require a choice or a yes-or-no answer, make gentle statements. For example, "Do you want dinner now?" might be rephrased as, "The clock shows it's time to have dinner now." Whenever possible, try to transform chores into joint games; you might say, "Let's see how fast we can get the toys into that box" when cleanup time comes. If the child resists in spite of your best strategies, do not let yourself get locked into a battle. It is better simply to abandon the dispute — by changing activities or by walking away into another room, perhaps. In cases when it is absolutely necessary to override the youngster's

wishes, you should do so firmly and swiftly, without argument.

The two-year-old's vocabulary expands to nearly a thousand words by year's end, and he loves stories, books, nursery rhymes and conversation. But he does not always fully understand what he is saying when he declares that something is true or makes a solemn promise.

Most two-year-olds are in the process of toilet training *(page 115)*, first for bowel movements, then urination. Handle toileting matter-of-factly, without extravagant praise and certainly without criticism. At bedtime *(page 116)*, many children follow set rituals, which the parents can explain to you beforehand. Once the child is tucked into bed, firmly resist any pleas for further attention, with one exception: The two-year-old's active imagination may create terrifying bogeymen at bedtime and sometimes nightmares as he sleeps. You should treat all such fears seriously, and do what you can to offer reassurance to the youngster. Sometimes a solution as simple as shutting the window will do the trick.

Three to Four Years

A preschooler of three occasionally may regress to two-year-old behavior, but in general she is more reasonable and easier to deal with now that she is a little older. While still quite self-centered, she is becoming aware of the concept of "we" and feels concern for the emotions of others. She takes a social interest in other children, playing with them and developing friendships. When disagreements arise, she generally is able to work out a compromise, such as sharing or taking turns, rather than fighting or crying.

Because of her growing imagination, the three-year-old delights in games of dress-up and make-believe. But sometimes the youngster is not quite sure where reality ends and fantasy begins. She may have imaginary friends, or she may pretend that she is an animal or another person. And a child this age can be terrified by fairy tales or violent television shows, which to her may seem quite real.

Perhaps in response to her changing and increasingly complex world, a three-year-old sometimes is quite conservative in her behavior and attitudes. She may be deeply concerned about doing things correctly, and she is often wedded to routines for dressing, meals and bedtime. You should be sensitive to and respect these comforting rituals. To avoid problems, give the child advance notice of your plans — for example, "We're going to eat dinner in five minutes."

Four to Five Years

At about the age of four, many children enter a stage marked by exuberant, boastful and assertive behavior. The older preschooler lives in a world of extremes: He has a passion for adventure, excursions, anything new, and he tends to dislike the things he dislikes just as intensely. Physically, he is apt to be found racing around the house, doing things with slap-dash speed and with little regard for perfection.

The child's play now often imitates the lives of real people, such as doctors, firefighters and astronauts. He may prefer playing with adult objects, such as flashlights and tools, rather than with toys: If you are in doubt about something of his parents' that he wants to play with, firmly tell him no. A child this age also enjoys collecting things.

The four-year-old usually delights in exaggeration and silliness. He likes fairy tales that tell of good and evil, of impossible feats and of mayhem. And he often weaves fictional ideas into descriptions of his own fantastic adventures. He will happily let you join in the exaggeration, or you can say, "Is that so?" and basically ignore the boasting.

During this year, the child respects rules and the structure they provide, although he sometimes may test the limits. You can avoid conflict by taking the positive approach — telling him what he should do rather than what he should not. Another good tactic is planning actions in advance, such as agreeing to go to bed at the end of a TV program. Misbehavior should be dealt with by stating the rule as a principle rather than giving a specific order: Say, "It's the rule that you don't hurt other people," not, "Don't strangle your sister."

A four-year-old often is interested in sexual differences, garbage, waste and elimination — and in joking about such matters. He may be secretive about bathroom functions; you should respect his privacy. He also may use swear words to shock adults, without knowing quite what he is saying. If you ignore foul language, chances are he will soon abandon it.

Five to Six Years

By the time she reaches kindergarten age, a youngster is basically self-sufficient. She can cut soft food with a knife and fork, dress and groom herself and tie her shoes. She speaks fluently and loves to tell her favorite stories. She knows the family's address and telephone number. And the youngster probably has mastered some school skills: She may be able to recite the alphabet, name several colors, print her name and count to 10 or 20.

Because the five-year-old is more autonomous, she may want to plan her own activities. As a sitter, you may need to become a playmate rather than a supervisor. Play often involves elaborate constructions — castles, forts and cities made of blocks. And since kindergartners enjoy bright colors, she may want to make brilliant paintings or drawings for you.

A five-year-old also usually likes social ceremonies, such as presenting and receiving gifts. She can recognize and express her own emotions, fears and anxieties — explaining, for example, "I'm afraid of that dog." Because she understands family rules and is eager to please, she needs your respect. She will resent babying. As she moves closer to six, however, she will want to assert more independence, and in the process her behavior may become bold and at times disobedient. This can be a difficult transition, for both parents and baby-sitters. But like the other stages the child has passed through, it is a natural and necessary part of growing up. ❖

Independent preschoolers can happily cruise the world on their own — by tricycle or afoot — but they still need a baby-sitter's watchful attention during their adventures. You should quietly stay close enough to protect the child from such hazards as cars, bicyclists, unfriendly dogs or the rough play of older children.

Helpful Hints on Basic Care

Feeding

A big part of many baby-sitting jobs is making sure a child is fed. Give yourself plenty of time to prepare food so it will be ready when he is hungry. That way you can sit down, relax and enjoy mealtime together. Here are some other suggestions:

- Ask the parents how to hold the baby for feeding during meals or how to use the high chair, how to prepare formula or other food, and what to do if the child fusses. Ask whether a toddler or an older child may have snacks. Find out how to use the stove and other kitchen appliances. Always follow parents' instructions exactly.

- Never carry a child in your arms while preparing food, and keep him away from the stove, garbage can, matches, appliances, sharp utensils and breakable objects.

- To warm a bottle of milk or formula, stand the bottle in a small saucepan containing three or four inches of water and heat it on a stove burner. Always test the milk or formula when you think it is ready: Sprinkle a few drops on your wrist — it should be warm, not hot.

- Heat soft foods by spooning them into a small saucepan and warming them over low heat. Test them on your wrist.

- Halfway through a bottle feeding — or if the baby fusses — try burping him for up to five minutes. Then feed him again. Unless he falls asleep during the feeding, burp him again at the end of the meal. To burp a baby, support him against your shoulder or in a sitting position on your lap. Then gently rub or pat his back. Keep a cloth handy in case he spits up a little food after burping or eating.

- Never leave a child in a room alone in an infant seat or a high chair, even if he is strapped in. And never prop a bottle for a baby if you must interrupt a feeding.

- An older child can help you prepare food and clean up as long as he observes the rules of kitchen safety. Or let him play somewhere within your sight. Preschoolers enjoy your companionship at mealtime.

- Never force a child of any age to eat.

A good position for bottle-feeding is sitting in a comfortable chair with your arm supported by the chair arm and the infant's head resting in the crook of your elbow. As he sucks, tilt the bottle so that he is swallowing only liquid, not air.

A toddler can get pretty messy at mealtimes. Be patient: He is learning to be independent. Let him try eating alone first and then offer help if he needs it. Give him only a little food at a time. You can always serve more. And you will have less to clean up later.

Diapering and Toileting

Changing a diaper or helping a toddler go to the bathroom may seem like the worst part of your job, but it is an important responsibility. You will do fine at it if you just remember to encourage a child and never to make her think anything about her body is disgusting. Here are some other tips:

- Ask questions: How often do the parents usually change their baby? What diapers, powder or ointment, and wiping cloth do they use? Where should you put dirty diapers? How should you help a toddler who is being toilet trained?

- A baby can wear a slightly wet diaper for a little while, but change her promptly if she has diaper rash. Change a soiled or very wet diaper right away.

- Change a child on a flat surface where you have placed an absorbent pad. If the surface does not have a strap you can fasten, always keep one hand on the child.

- Collect everything you need for changing before you start. Look at the old diaper before removing it to see how to fit the new one. Undo the diaper, then lift the child gently by the ankles with one hand and pull out the diaper with the other. Wipe her from front to back with a clean, damp cloth. Then position a new diaper and fasten it.

- Always keep safety pins closed and out of a child's reach. When sticking them through a cloth diaper, always put your hand between the diaper and the child's skin.

- Encourage a toddler who is being toilet trained by asking her how she uses the potty or by complimenting her when she keeps her pants dry.

- Take a child to the bathroom gently but quickly if she dances impatiently from foot to foot or gives you some other warning. Avoid forcing her if she refuses to go.

- Undo a child's clothing and lift her onto the potty if she wants or needs your help. Once she is finished, help her wipe herself, flush the toilet and get dressed again.

- If a toileting accident happens, be understanding.

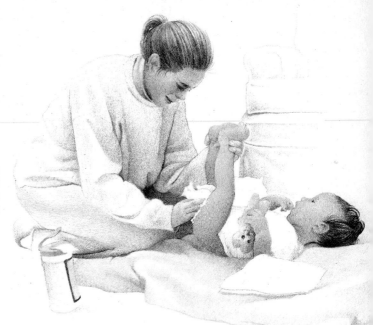

If you feel uneasy about handling a baby on a high changing table, you can put a pad on the floor and change his diaper there. To distract a restless, squirmy child long enough for you to get the job done, you might try giving him a toy to play with.

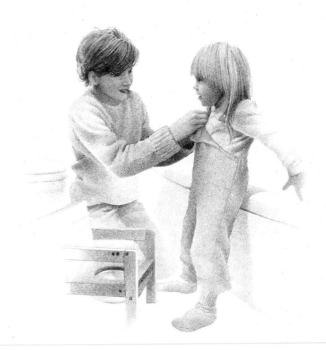

Remember that a newly toilet-trained toddler may need help in the bathroom with snaps, zippers and other fasteners. But be tactful about offering your assistance. Many youngsters this age are also going through the "me do it myself" stage of growing independence and often insist on doing everything themselves.

Bedtime

Baby-sitting can be especially challenging at bedtime. Many children go to sleep without any problems; others dream up every trick imaginable to avoid the crib or the bed. You cannot force a child to sleep — but you can try to understand why he is avoiding it. Here is some advice:

- Always ask parents about a child's sleeping habits. What position does the baby sleep in? Is there an important bedtime routine, such as reading certain books? Write down the parents' instructions if you need to.

- A baby usually sleeps a lot. Change him into a clean diaper just before bedtime. Spend a few quiet minutes with him after turning out the lights — you might sing, rock him or stroke him gently. If he wakes up later and does not fall back asleep within 10 minutes, try rocking, burping, or walking with him before you try feeding. If nothing works, just hold him — or call his parents.

- Feed a toddler or an older child way ahead of bedtime. Put him in his nightclothes early, then let him play quietly or do something else he really enjoys. Avoid rough play and scary TV shows. Mention the idea of sleeping early on so the youngster can prepare for it and then give him another little reminder just before bedtime.

- Do not compromise if a child keeps getting out of bed. Just take him back, soothe him again and say good night. Repeat this routine again and again until it works.

- Go immediately to a child who seems to be having nightmares. Never laugh or make fun of him. Comfort him by sitting on the bed, holding him, tucking him in or singing softly. Or tell him you know how scary bad dreams can be and let the youngster come sit by you with his blanket and favorite toy until he gets sleepy.

- Check on a sleeping child every 30 to 45 minutes, and make sure nothing is covering his head. Keep the TV or music turned down so you will hear him if he cries. And you should never leave a child alone in the house — not even when he is sleeping.

To keep bedtime as struggle-free as possible, be sure to follow carefully any special rituals or routines the child is accustomed to — whether it is a bedtime story, a favorite animal to cuddle or a night light to keep the monsters away. Once the child is in bed, let her know gently but firmly that she must stay there.

Crying and Comforting

All children cry now and then. Sometimes they are hungry or thirsty. Or they might be tired and irritable. Maybe they are lonely and miss their parents. Whatever the reason, it is up to you to soothe them. These suggestions may help:

- Find out from the parents what position their baby likes to be held in and if thumb-sucking or giving a pacifier is okay. Also ask if the baby or toddler is teething and if you should give her teething medication.

- Check the obvious when a child is crying: hunger, thirst, sleepiness, boredom, overstimulation. These are all things that you can easily fix.

- A small baby often screams to tell you that something hurts or she is uncomfortable. Maybe an open safety pin is poking her in the side. Or perhaps she needs burping. Check her diaper and make sure her clothing is not too loose or tight. Check her temperature by touching her neck.

- Wrapping a baby in a blanket, gently dancing with her in your arms, making soothing sounds and playing soft music are a few of the ways you might calm an infant. If nothing works, take a break for a few minutes and try again. If she feels feverish or seems otherwise sick, call her parents.

- Let a teething baby or toddler chew on a clean teething ring or rubber toy. You can also rub her sore gums gently with a very clean finger.

- Never laugh at a toddler or an older child if she is scared of something. Instead, treat it seriously. You might blow monsters out the window, leave a night light or hall light on, or hold her during a thunderstorm.

- Never take crying personally. Just stay relaxed and calm — otherwise a baby or child might sense you are upset and as a result cry even harder.

- If the crying goes on and on but you are not sure why, call the parents or at least tell them about it later. And be optimistic: The more you baby-sit, the better you will get at comforting children of all ages.

Babies are not the only ones who cry. You will often be called on to give your sympathetic attention to an older child who suffers a bump or a scrape or an emotional disappointment. Never ridicule or brush aside a child who is upset; instead, listen to his story and try to help him see ways to make himself feel better.

Discipline

Baby-sitting would be a breeze if children were as mature as you are. But young children cannot yet completely control their impulses and feelings or explain what is bothering them. Sometimes when they are unable to express themselves in words, they scream, cry, hit, even bite to get their way. Children who behave this way are just acting their age. It is also natural for youngsters to make a mess, run around wildly and insist stubbornly on doing everything by themselves. Once you have had some baby-sitting experience, you will learn special ways of handling each child. Here are some tips:

- Stay calm but watchful and fast on your feet. Avoid making an issue of every minor incident, as long as no one is hurt.

- A child who misbehaves is probably trying to get your attention. The best way to prevent this is to reinforce positive behavior by giving him lots of attention when he is behaving well and is doing what you want him to do.

- Ask parents how they discipline their child. Always report any bad language or behavior to parents but never do so in front of the child.

- Stick to reasonable rules and limits. If a child insists on doing something unwise, either figure out a safe way to do it or persuade him that another activity would be more fun. Let him do as much for himself as possible.

- When a child misbehaves, never spank, punish, lecture, yell or withdraw your affection as punishment. Instead, look directly into his eyes and speak in a friendly but firm, low-pitched voice. Use positive phrases such as "let's try" instead of negatives such as "you can't."

- Give an older child choices instead of asking questions he can answer with a loud "No!" For example, instead of asking if he wants milk, ask if he wants it in a mug or a glass.

- Let a child know you will never contradict his parents' wishes. If he tries to trick or upset you, just ignore it. Otherwise he may begin to feel that he can control the situation with such tactics.

If children are arguing, let them work it out or suggest a compromise, but never take sides. Break up the fight immediately, however, if you think that someone may get hurt, and have the children play separately until they are ready to get along.

Tantrums

Children have tantrums when they are so upset that the only outlet for their feelings is an explosion. They might be angry or hurt, lonely or scared, hungry or tired. Maybe they simply cannot cope with decisions or pressures that are weighing on them. Whatever the reason, a deeply frustrated child can become an explosive little bundle — one you have to defuse quickly before a blowup occurs. Here are some suggestions:

- Avoid putting too many restrictions on a child and make sure she knows how you expect her to behave.

- Try to sense when a child's limits have been reached and then do something to change the situation. For example, calm down a child who is getting overexcited or feed her if you see she is getting cranky from hunger. And make sure she is having fun doing things she wants to do without unnecessary interference.

- Try to stay calm and ignore a child's tantrums. Why? Because throwing a fit is no fun at all if nobody is watching.

- Try making friendly gestures during a tantrum. A hug or an offer to play shows a child that you are not angry. You might even offer to make her a snack if the parents have said that eating between meals is okay.

- During a ferocious tantrum, try saying or doing something silly or whispering, so that the child has to stop screaming to hear you. You might also try putting her in bed, on a couch or in some other comfortable place with a cozy blanket or a favorite stuffed animal, and then simply letting the tantrum blow over.

- If a child still seems angry once a tantrum ends, you might dance, exercise, jump or play active games together to help her work off that anger.

- If a child has two or more tantrums every time you babysit, discuss it with her parents. Try to figure out what the problem is and how you might be able to help. Remember, too, that tantrums decrease as children grow older.

While it is best not to reward a child's temper tantrums by paying a lot of attention, do let her know that you are standing nearby in case you are needed. You must make sure that no one gets hurt and nothing gets broken during the outburst.

Safety Guidelines

Preventing Accidents Indoors

Like a lifeguard, a baby-sitter is responsible above all for the children's safety. You can begin by enforcing any family rules the parents have set forth. But you also must be alert for unforeseen problems. Here is a check list of safety precautions:

- When you arrive at the house, survey the emergency exits. Ask the parents which doors and windows are locked and where the keys are kept.

- Ask the parents which rooms are off-limits, then keep their doors or gates shut. Do not let the child play in the garage, basement, storage room, bathroom or kitchen, all of which are full of hidden hazards.

- Do not let a child out of your sight unless you are sure he cannot get into trouble. Children younger than five should never be left alone, except in a crib, playpen or bed.

- Remove fire hazards. Know where to find fire extinguishers and how to use them, but do not use an extinguisher for anything larger than a smoldering wastebasket. If a real fire breaks out, take the child and leave the house immediately; call the fire department from a neighbor's phone.

- Prevent poisoning by watching closely what the child is playing with or handling. Many ordinary items are potential poisons — including house plants, under-the-sink detergents, vitamin pills, and medicines from your purse or book bag.

- Be especially watchful in the kitchen. Keep knives, cords and appliances out of reach. Use the stove's back burners and turn pot handles inward, so that a child cannot reach them. Check stove and oven controls before leaving the kitchen.

- To prevent falls, carry the child with two hands and strap him into his high chair. Keep crib rails and playpen sides raised. And whenever a baby is placed at any height — on a couch, bed or changing table, for example — keep one hand on him. Otherwise he can roll or crawl over the edge in a moment. With older children, forbid running near stairways, balconies and open windows.

- Keep the child away from electric sockets or cords.

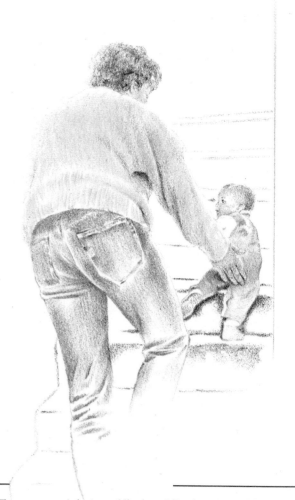

To protect a stair-loving toddler from falls, always stay on his downhill side: Follow behind him as he climbs up stairs and go ahead of him on the way down. Keep the stairway clear of toys and other objects he could stumble on. And when you carry a child on the stairs, always hold onto the railing.

Precautions for Outdoor Play

Children love to go outside. But in the great outdoors, a child and her environment both are difficult to control. Get a parent's approval for the expedition and its destination before you set out, even for a short walk. Then follow these guidelines:

- Dress the child appropriately; young children are especially vulnerable to extremes of sun, heat and cold. In summer, apply sunscreen if the child will be exposed to the sun for very long; you might also wish to protect her face with a hat or cap. In winter, dress the child in layers of clothing.

- Stay within a few feet of the child, so that you can reach her easily if she runs away or approaches something dangerous.

- If you use a stroller, strap the child in and never leave the stroller unattended.

- Be particularly careful near traffic. When crossing a street, hold the child's hand or carry her. If the child is playing near a roadway, stay between the child and the traffic.

- Do not let the child put into her mouth foreign objects such as dirt, sticks, stones, plants and grass.

- Watch out for broken glass, nails and other sharp objects.

- Keep the child away from animals, except for family pets.

- Stay away from abandoned appliances.

- Do not let the child play in or on unstable structures, such as a rickety homemade fort, or ditches, tunnels, sand piles, construction sites or abandoned houses.

- When the child plays in or near water — even a large puddle — do not take your eyes off her, even if a lifeguard is present. Do not let the child play in water over your own head unless you are a strong swimmer. And never allow the child near an unattended swimming pool, empty or full.

- Do not let the child play near an unfenced body of water, such as a pond, creek, river, aqueduct or irrigation ditch. Hold her hand when passing such hazards.

To guide a child away from playground hazards such as the swing above, stay within easy reach of her so that you can steer her clear of an accident. Be especially watchful near moving equipment such as swings, merry-go-rounds and seesaws. Equally important, you should keep the child away from the rough, fast-moving games of older children.

Keeping Kids Busy and Entertained

A little advance preparation can go a long way toward making a baby-sitting job more fun for you and more rewarding for your charges. For example, some sitters bring a surprise bag or box supplied with toys and materials for games and crafts. An old toolbox, purse or drawstring bag makes a good container. Other sitters prefer to ask parents ahead of time for the items they need for planned activities. On the following pages you will find a brief description of children's interests and abilities at various ages, along with suggested playthings and activities appropriate for youngsters from birth through six years.

Birth to Six Months

Newborn babies sleep a lot, but when they are awake they like to be kept warm and cozy and have someone take care of their physical needs. From the earliest weeks, a baby pays attention to what is going on around him. From three to six months, babies are all eyes and ears — and fingers and mouth, as well — so they enjoy activities that stimulate their senses. By four months, a baby can play for as long as an hour at a time.

Playthings for This Age

Rattles; a music box; a stuffed animal; a brightly colored cloth ball or one with indentations for little fingers to explore.

Suggested Activities

● Make a hand puppet that can talk to the baby by decorating a sock with a felt-tip marker. Push the toe between your fingers and thumb to make the mouth and wiggle your fingers as you talk to make the puppet come alive.

● When the baby babbles, imitate his sounds and then listen as he babbles back. Keep the conversation going. Babbling is the beginning of language; your imitation will encourage him to continue.

● Play peekaboo, hiding a toy animal under a diaper or baby blanket. Say, "Where's Teddy?" and as you whip off the cover call out, "Peekaboo!"

● Even the youngest babies will enjoy rattle play with you. Hold the rattle and move it so that the baby can follow it with his eyes. Hold it in front of him, within his reach, and let him bat at it or grab it. At about three months, he can hold it and play with it by himself.

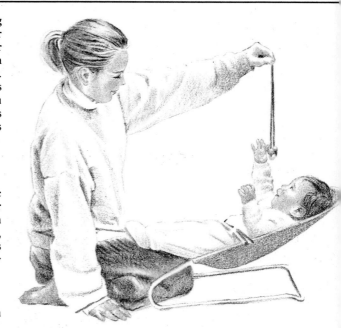

Babies love to bat at objects that are dangled in front of them, as this infant is doing with his sitter's necklace. Each time the child swats at the colorful beads, he is practicing eye-hand coordination. But be careful never to allow a baby to grab and hold anything he might swallow or choke on, or a string that might cause strangulation.

Six to 12 Months

Now the baby is beginning to understand a few words and will enjoy simple wordplay. She is likely to listen intently while you talk to her or point to things and name them. Pat-a-cake and other rhymes that you remember from your childhood will delight her. She is eager to imitate gestures of those around her, and she will enjoy mirror games.

Playthings for This Age

Plastic measuring cups or other containers that she can stack and unstack; picture books with simple stories or nursery rhymes, magazines and catalogues; unbreakable dishes, cups and saucers; toys with wheels; squeak toys and bells.

Suggested Activities

- To play an affectionate game of chase that many crawling babies love, follow the child around the room on all fours, eventually catching and hugging her.

- Babies this age also like to play imitation games. When you see the child waving her hand or patting the table, for ex-ample, repeat what she does. Soon she will catch on.

- Take turns making funny faces and funny sounds with her in front of a mirror. Show her simple actions such as wrinkling the nose or changing from a smile to a frown. Point to her eyes, nose and mouth and name them. Let her brush her hair using her own comb and brush.

- The baby will enjoy looking at books, magazines or catalogues while you name the things in the pictures.

- Show the child a squeak toy and squeeze it to make the sound, then hide it under furniture or a blanket. Squeak it again and help the baby find it by following the sound.

- Set the baby on the floor, legs spread apart, while you sit facing her the same way a few feet away. Roll a beach ball toward her so that it goes between her legs and encourage her to roll it back to you. If you are taking care of more than one child, this is a game that can include all of them.

Most babies are delighted by a gentle blanket ride along a tiled or wooden floor. Place the child on her tummy in the middle of a blanket and pull her slowly, with smooth stops and starts, being careful not to bump into anything. Games with lots of movement, such as this one, should be followed by quiet activities.

One-Year-Olds

Toddlers between one and two years old seem to be constantly running and climbing and probably will enjoy chasing you around the room. They fall down frequently but rarely injure themselves; you usually can kiss a hurt to make it better and go on with the game. They understand most of what you are saying, so they like word games. And many toddlers love to scribble with crayons on paper.

Playthings for This Age

Toys that can be pulled or pushed across the floor; picture books; an indoor sponge ball; cardboard tubes; maracas, drum or other rhythm instruments; large crayons.

Suggested Activities

- The singing and finger games you may remember from your own early childhood are favorites with children of this age. Perhaps you remember singing to the tune of *Frère Jacques,* "Where is Thumbkin? Where is Thumbkin? Here I am, here I am," and holding up your thumb as Thumbkin answers. The song continues with "How are you this morning? Very fine, I thank you. I am fine." It then asks "Where is Elbow?" — and so on, through the parts of the body.

- Play a recording of children's songs while you and your charge march around beating rhythm instruments. If there are no real instruments available, tap a metal pot or a cardboard box with a spoon.

- You can make a game out of imitating sounds familiar to the child. Start with a sound you have just heard, perhaps a dog barking or a fire engine siren, and continue through a group of sounds, for example, a plane zooming or a bee buzzing. Accompany the sounds with actions.

- Read nursery rhymes and short, rhyming stories aloud.

- Make sounds through a cardboard tube — whispering, singing or shouting. Try tubes of different sizes.

- Play hide-and-seek. Hide in places where you will be easy to find, such as behind the sofa, and leave some part of yourself in view until the child gets the idea. Do not stay hidden if the youngster does not find you right away.

Ask your young charge, "How big is Tommy?" Then demonstrate an answer by stretching your hands as high as you can and saying, "So big." Get him to mimic the action and words. Try variations such as, "How quiet is Tommy?" (He whispers, "So quiet.") "How fast is Tommy?" (He answers as he runs.)

Two-Year-Olds

Two-year-olds are strong-willed and will eagerly show you what book they want read to them or what toy they want to play with. They like to hear their favorite stories again and again. They enjoy building simple block structures. They can spend long stretches of time drawing happily — providing you do not pressure them to produce pictures. Instead, let them enjoy the colors and the sense of control that drawing gives them. Spread old newspapers beneath the paper on which they are drawing, so you do not have to worry about stray marks on the table. Watch to see that crayons and felt-tip markers do not end up in mouths and do not mark on walls.

Playthings for This Age

Felt-tip markers and paper; masks; storybooks; puppets; an easy puzzle; a large cardboard box; blocks; costume box with ties, hats, purses, scarves, shoes; party hats; tape recorder.

Suggested Activities

- The nursery rhymes that appeal to a child this age are those accompanied by strong actions, such as "Pop Goes the Weasel," "Ring Around the Rosie" and "London Bridge Is Falling Down." These rhymes are even more fun if you can include more than one child.

- Your charge has probably begun enjoying birthday parties and might like to celebrate a pretend one with her favorite dolls and animals. Let her decide which doll has a birthday and then let her help you wrap some toys as presents. Create a pretend cake from a cupcake, cookie or piece of bread. You can make party hats by rolling sheets of paper decorated with felt-tip markers into cone shapes, and then securing each hat with staples.

- Ask the child to sing or talk into the microphone of a cassette tape recorder, then play it back for her. Take turns talking into it and encourage her to expand what she says. Let her press the buttons to record and play the tapes.

- Play dress-up. Join the child in putting on old hats, ties, purses, shoes and scarves, and then parade with her in front of a mirror. And try the effect of different masks.

You can make simple puzzles from cardboard. On each piece draw a large square, semicircle or triangle, using a ruler for the straight lines. Color the shapes with felt-tip markers and then cut them out. Show the child how each one fits into the piece it was cut from. The first shapes should have one straight side that forms an outside edge of the cardboard, but as the child gets used to doing the puzzles, you can cut the shapes from the center.

To make a cape, use a rectangular piece of fabric approximately 12 inches wide by 18 inches long. Twist the two top corners and tie a length of yarn around each of them. Draw a butterfly or any other design on the fabric with felt-tip markers. The youngster will love running around with the cape fanning out behind her as she soars into her own imaginary adventures.

125

Three-Year-Olds

A child this age is developing new skills rapidly and is eager for challenges that stretch his abilities. He can throw and catch balls. His drawings are beginning to represent real life as he makes a sun, a tree or stick people with a few details of clothing. When he hears music, he wants to dance, march or beat time. He enjoys stories that feature active children like himself ·as well as curious monkeys, happy lions, loyal elephants and persevering train engines.

Playthings for This Age

Beanbags, bubble pipes, magnets, rhythm instruments, non-toxic modeling clay or play dough, paper cups, crayons, felt-tip markers, coloring books, construction paper, paper grocery bags, child's safety scissors, shoe boxes, chalk and chalkboard, poster paints and brushes.

Suggested Activities

● Make a raceway for the youngster's cars on the carpet by lining up a number of books of equal thickness. Let him help you choose the books by matching thicknesses. Be sure to remember where you got the books so you can put them away properly later.

● A child can gallop along on a broomstick pony he helps you make. Stuff a sock with newspaper and tie the open end onto a broomstick or yardstick. Draw eyes and a mouth on the sock with a felt-tip marker; glue on pointed ears made of construction paper and a mane of bright-colored yarn.

● Get the child to help you make a carnival-style throwing game out of paper cups and some aluminum foil. Stack upside-down paper cups into a pyramid on a shoe box: a row of four cups on the bottom, three on top of that, then two and one at the top. Show him how to crumple clean foil into a ball and throw it to try to knock down the cups.

● Show your charge how to make pictures of coins by rubbing. Place a piece of typing paper over a quarter. Rub the paper lightly with the lead of a pencil. You will see the design of the quarter emerge on the paper. Let the child do the same for other coins — a nickel, dime and penny. The same kind of rubbings can be made using leaves.

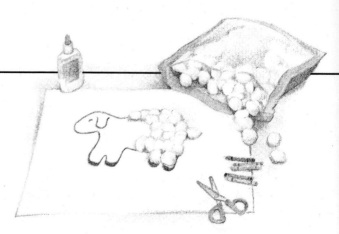

Help the child create a lamb with a "pet me" feel. Draw a lamb on construction paper and let him fill in the outline with nontoxic glue. Show him how cotton balls will stick to the glue and have him cover the drawing with the fluffy white balls.

A large paper grocery bag can become a clown costume for pretend play. In advance, cut colored construction paper into such shapes as hats, hearts, flowers, circles and stars. Cut large armholes, eyeholes and a mouth hole in the paper bag. Then let the child decorate the bag with felt-tip markers and paints, and by gluing on yarn, cotton balls and the cutouts you made.

Four-Year-Olds

Imaginative games that imitate adult activities occupy much of the playtime of four-year-olds. Your charge probably enjoys books about people and their jobs, as well as fairy tales. She can build fairly elaborate structures with interlocking blocks and is ready for games such as Simon Says, which require following instructions.

Playthings for This Age

Interlocking building blocks, magnetic alphabet letters, storybooks, puzzles of eight to 20 pieces, large cartons, large balls, colored chalk, dress-up clothes, construction paper, pipe cleaners, lunch-size paper bags, felt-tip markers and crayons, child's safety scissors, child's portable slide viewer, colorful scarves, stickers and poster board.

Suggested Activities

- Make a face that lights up. Trace the circumference of a flashlight on the bottom of a thin paper bag. Let the child draw a face in the circle with a black crayon. Fit the bag over the flashlight and secure it with a rubber band. When you turn out the lights and switch on the flashlight, the face on the bag will light up on the wall or ceiling.

- Colored chalk creates interesting effects on paper when one or the other is wet. Dampen the construction paper and then let the child draw on it with chalk.

- Help your charge make a book. Put a few sheets of paper together and fold the whole sheaf in half so it opens like a book. You may want to staple it at the fold. Let the child tell you about one of her experiences, perhaps a visit to a supermarket. Together, draw pictures that illustrate events in the order in which they happened. Then let her "read" the book aloud to you.

- The child will enjoy playing imaginative games with you — house, store, police or school — where you dress up and use actual household items such as pots and unopened cans of food. The space under a table makes a cozy home, office or firehouse. If you line up a few chairs, you can make a car or bus that she will want to drive. A large carton can be her boat; several large cartons lined up make a train.

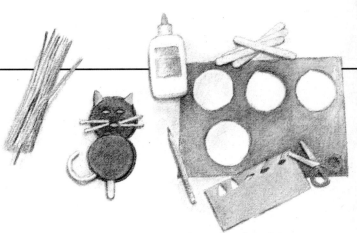

To make a black cat stick puppet, cut four circles of equal size from black construction paper. Glue two of the circles to both sides of the top of a wooden ice-cream stick to make the cat's head, and the other two just below, overlapping the first circles a little, for the cat's body. Glue on eyes, ears and a mouth cut from colored paper, and add whiskers and a tail made from white pipe cleaners. You can make other animals by changing the body shapes, ears and tail.

Create a princess's hat such as those in the pictures in fairy-tale books. Roll a sheet of poster board into a cone and staple or tape the ends together. Trim the open end of the cone so that it will fit the child's head. Punch holes through both sides near the point. Help the youngster thread a colorful scarf through the holes and then let her decorate the cone with stickers.

Five-year-olds

Children this age are capable of many skillful activities, including cutting out shapes using a child's safety scissors. Sometimes they like to repeat an activity again and again until they get it right. Five-year-olds are expressive in their dancing and love learning new steps. They enjoy collecting such things as coins or rocks. Myths, legends and folk tales are among their favorite stories. And they are ready for card games such as old maid and go fish.

Playthings for This Age

Marbles, cardboard boxes of different sizes and shapes, milk cartons, cardboard tubes, deck of cards, child's safety scissors, crayons and felt-tip markers, paper plates, poster board, construction paper, magazines that can be cut up, small jars of ornamental glitter and egg cartons.

Suggested Activities

● Help the child build a city with cardboard boxes of different sizes. He can decorate the buildings with felt-tip markers or crayons, and add cardboard-tube or milk-carton towers. Ask the child to remember places he has been in the city, such as the school or the post office, and then see whether the two of you can make a model of it.

● Make up silly stories together. Start a sentence and break it off where the child can continue it with his own ideas. Keep the story going by taking turns adding new twists.

● Challenge the child with a treasure hunt. Hide one of his toys. Give him clues that will help him find it, such as "not higher than your shoulder or lower than your knee," or "in a soft place." Tell him when he is hot or cold. When he finds it, let him hide something and give you clues.

● Use magazine pictures to steer the child's attention to new ideas for his artwork. Cut a circular section from the center of an interesting magazine or catalogue picture and paste it in the middle of a blank sheet of drawing paper. With the center portion in place to get him started, suggest that the youngster complete the picture.

Paper plates can make funny, decorative and useful items. Help the child cut a wedge out of a paper plate to make a fish's mouth. She can draw a face on her fish with felt-tip markers. Then staple the cut-out triangle into place as a tail. Or show her how to cut a paper plate in half and staple a half-plate to a second paper plate. After decorating it, the child will have a mail pouch for special notes or pictures.

The child can make a trace-and-paste collage such as this using ordinary objects found around the house and yard — leaves, coins, keys, a small box, clothespins or utensils — for patterns. Have him trace the items onto colored construction paper, cut out his tracings and glue them onto white poster board.

Goofy goggles such as these add the finishing touch to any costume. Cut out two connected sections of an egg carton. Cut holes in the center of each cup so that the child can see through them. Also punch small holes through the sides of the cups; then insert pipe cleaners and bend them to form earpieces. Let the youngster decorate the silly goggles with felt-tip markers.

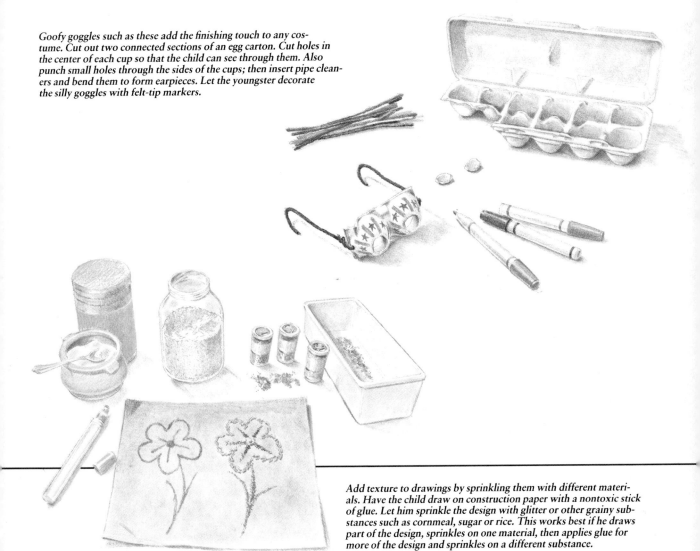

Add texture to drawings by sprinkling them with different materials. Have the child draw on construction paper with a nontoxic stick of glue. Let him sprinkle the design with glitter or other grainy substances such as cornmeal, sugar or rice. This works best if he draws part of the design, sprinkles on one material, then applies glue for more of the design and sprinkles on a different substance.

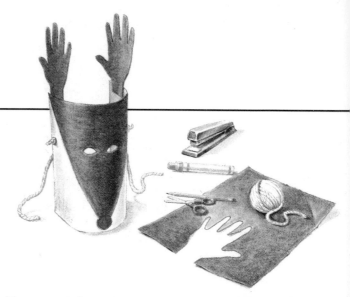

Six-Year-Olds

You will be delighted with the independence and reliability of most six-year-olds. Their longer attention span enables them to do a wide variety of crafts. Outdoors, they like to jump rope, do simple calisthenics, play hopscotch, hide-and-seek, and running games such as tag. Inside, they enjoy pencil-and-paper games such as ticktacktoe. Your charge may be able to read stories to you, too.

Playthings for This Age

Kite, ring-toss game, magnifying glass, poster paints, checkers, table-tennis balls, flash cards, jump rope, clothespins, pencils, crayons, felt-tip markers, poster board, construction and wrapping paper, child's safety scissors, play dough, nut shells and magazines that can be cut up.

Suggested Activities

- Make 10 finger puppets by placing a peanut shell on each of the child's fingers after she draws eyes, noses and mouths on the shells with a felt-tip marker. Show her how to move her fingers to make the puppets dance, bob and bow, while she sings and talks.

- Let your charge invent a new food and design a new package for it. Glue paper onto an empty cereal box to cover the printing, then help her write and draw a new label. She might want to use her own name for the new product — for example, Marsha's Mishmash. You could put her photo or a picture she draws of herself on the label.

- A six-year-old can model aluminum foil like clay, rolling it into a cylinder and pinching or twisting it into people, animals or whatever shapes please her.

- Ask her parents if you and the child may look through their family album. She will enjoy pointing out friends and family members and telling you about them.

- For more active indoor play, place walnuts, clothespins, pencils or other small objects on the floor about two feet apart and let the youngster hop over them. She should move on only one foot at a time, but she can change feet if she gets tired. For an added challenge, have her pick up the objects as she hops by.

To create a reindeer mask, trace the child's hands and wrists on a piece of brown construction paper. Then draw a 10-inch-wide triangle on the same paper. Let her cut out those shapes and a round nose from red paper. Show her how to glue the triangle and the nose to an 8½-by-11-inch poster board, as shown above. Cut eyeholes about halfway down the triangle and poke holes through the poster board for yarn ties. Staple the hand-shape antlers in place and then tie the reindeer mask on the child.

Help the child make a life-size self-portrait. While she lies on a large sheet of paper, trace her outline. Let her fill in the features and colors. She can glue on yarn for hair and make a shirt from a remnant of fabric or wrapping paper. Cut around the outline of the figure when the youngster has finished it.

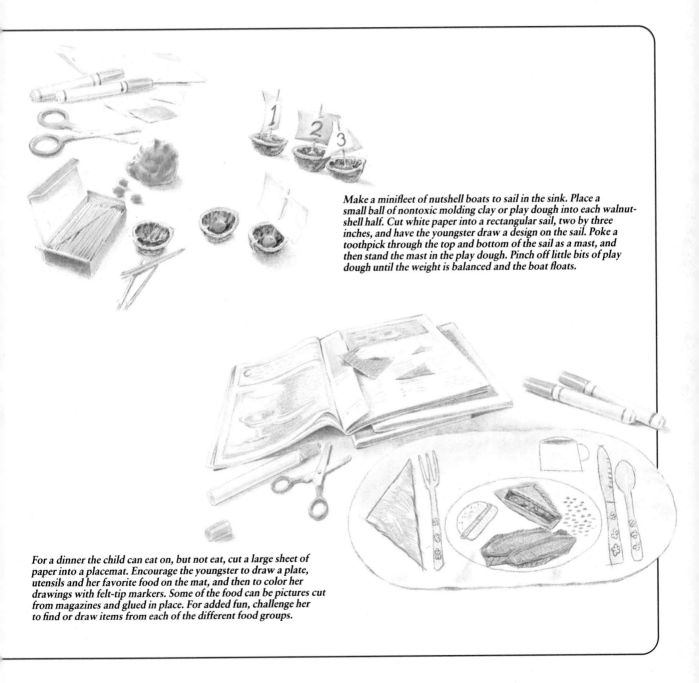

Make a minifleet of nutshell boats to sail in the sink. Place a small ball of nontoxic molding clay or play dough into each walnut-shell half. Cut white paper into a rectangular sail, two by three inches, and have the youngster draw a design on the sail. Poke a toothpick through the top and bottom of the sail as a mast, and then stand the mast in the play dough. Pinch off little bits of play dough until the weight is balanced and the boat floats.

For a dinner the child can eat on, but not eat, cut a large sheet of paper into a placemat. Encourage the youngster to draw a plate, utensils and her favorite food on the mat, and then to color her drawings with felt-tip markers. Some of the food can be pictures cut from magazines and glued in place. For added fun, challenge her to find or draw items from each of the different food groups.

Medical Concerns

Handling Illnesses and Accidents

As a baby-sitter, you will probably not have to deal with medical problems more serious than bumps, bruises and colds. But part of the job is being prepared to handle minor illnesses and accidents and even emergencies, such as bleeding and choking *(pages 134-135)*. Make sure you know where to find phone numbers for the fire department, the rescue squad and the poison-control center. Know how to give directions to the house. Know where to reach the child's parents. And know the location of the family's first-aid kit.

Do what you can to prevent problems, particularly with medicines. Do not give a child any medicine — not even aspirin — without his parents' permission. If the parents ask you to give medicine while they are gone, write down the exact instructions. Just before giving the dose, reread the instructions and read the medicine's label. If you are carrying any medicines of your own in a purse or book bag, keep them out of the child's reach.

If you do encounter a medical problem — anything from a minor scrape to life-threatening breathing trouble — the first step always is to pause for a few seconds and calmly evaluate the situation. Do not rush: Do things slowly and correctly.

The second step is to take whatever immediate action is needed. As you work, comfort the frightened child with sympathetic words and your own calmness. You may need to be firm with a crying, panicked child, but you should keep providing gentle reassurance — even in grave emergencies.

The third step is to call for help and advice. Never try to handle by yourself a medical problem that requires anything more than a simple adhesive bandage. Usually you can just notify the child's parents by telephone — for instance, to say that he has a fever or a cut. If you cannot reach the parents, call your own parents, the child's doctor, a hospital emergency room or a trusted neighbor. When the problem seems serious — if the child has convulsions, perhaps, or a head injury — do not hesitate to call the rescue squad. Then notify the parents.

Every baby-sitter should make sure to know first aid for a few common medical problems:

- Abrasions. Gently wash the raw, bleeding area with soap and running water, using sterile gauze pads to remove from the wound any embedded dirt. Dry the wound with gauze, then apply antibiotic ointment and a sterile bandage.

- Bruises. Ease the pain and swelling of minor bruises by cooling the area with an ice pack or with ice cubes wrapped in a washcloth for about 20 minutes. Do not use the ice pack for more than 20 minutes and never apply ice directly to the skin: This can cause frostbite. You should call the parents to report bruises that are large and swollen or extremely painful, that prevent movement of the affected part or that involve the fingernail, toenail or face.

- Insect stings. Wash the area with soap and water, then apply an ice pack for 20 minutes *(see Bruises)*. Honeybees leave stingers, which should be removed carefully with tweezers before you wash the wound. On rare occasions, stings cause dangerous allergic reactions, particularly among children with other allergies or with asthma. Call for help immediately if the child develops such symptoms as facial tingling or flushing, weakness, difficulty swallowing, a skin rash, itchy skin, rapid swelling or difficulty breathing.

- Vomiting and diarrhea. Clean up the child promptly, then tend to the mess, changing clothes and bed linens if necessary. Notify the parents if there is more than one episode, if the child complains of pain or queasiness, if the vomit or stool looks odd, or if vomit shoots more than one foot from the child's mouth.

- Poisoning. Keep a close watch over all young children, but especially toddlers from one to three years old, who will put anything in their mouths. Suspect poisoning if the child abruptly behaves oddly, becomes suddenly weak or sleepy, has trouble seeing, or develops vomiting, diarrhea or convulsions. Other signs to be on the lookout for are stains or burns around the mouth, or open containers of medicine or poisons. If you suspect poisoning, do not wait for proof: You should call the poison-control center at once. Except on the center's instructions, do not try to make the child vomit and do not give her anything to eat or drink. Save the container of suspected poison and any vomit the child produces.

- Convulsions. Remove nearby furniture and put a pillow under the child's head to prevent injury during the seizure. You should not restrain the child or put anything in her mouth. Call the rescue squad. Although seizures always require a doctor's evaluation, among children between the ages of one and five, they are not uncommon at the beginning of feverish illnesses.

- Head injuries. If after banging her head the youngster becomes sleepy, behaves oddly, bleeds from the ears or nose, or complains of headache, dizziness or double vision, you should call the emergency rescue squad immediately.

How to Stop Bleeding

Of all the medical problems that you may encounter while baby-sitting, bloody wounds are among the most common — and occasionally the scariest. Do not panic. Although a few tablespoons of spilled blood may look like a gallon, actually the human body has plenty of extra blood. Your job is to stop the bleeding, then to decide whether to call the rescue squad.

The key to stopping bleeding is direct pressure. Grab a sterile gauze pad, a towel, a handkerchief or any other clean cloth, and press it over the cut. If the cloth becomes soaked, do not remove it; put another pad on top and increase the pressure. For limb wounds, watch the hand or foot for signs of poor circulation; blue nails or cold skin means that you should ease the pressure a bit.

A few situations require special treatment. If the child has a nosebleed, have her sit and lean forward over a bowl or sink, with her chin down so that blood will not run down her throat. Then gently pinch the bottom of her nostrils together and hold them closed for at least five minutes, or until the bleeding stops. If the child is impaled by something — a nail or a fishhook, perhaps — do not remove the object; apply pressure around it and call for help.

Once you are applying pressure, pause to think. Did bright red blood pulse rhythmically from the wound (a sign of arterial bleeding)? Is substantial bleeding continuing despite your pressure? Has the child lost much blood? Is she pale, clammy, sweaty or cold (signs of shock)? If the answer to any of these questions is yes, maintain the pressure and call the rescue squad, even if the bleeding stops. Otherwise maintain pressure for five to 10 minutes, then cautiously remove the pad. Should the bleeding resume, apply direct pressure and summon the child's parents, your parents or a trusted neighbor to drive the child to a doctor or to an emergency room.

If the bleeding has stopped or slowed to an ooze, look carefully at the wound's location, depth and edges. Then report to the parents. Most cuts can be treated with adhesive bandages or with gauze. But some wounds always need a doctor's attention: These include facial cuts, a cut that is deep or wide, any wound that is dirty or has broken glass in it, and animal bites. If medical care is needed, seek it promptly; the risk of infection increases with every hour of delay, and wounds cannot safely be stitched after about six hours.

To stop severe bleeding in an injured limb, raise the wound higher than the heart and apply firm, direct pressure with a clean cloth pad. Do not raise the limb if a bone is broken.

What to Do for Choking

Children under five years old can choke on virtually any small object — a plastic bag, a small toy, a piece of food. As a baby-sitter you can do much to prevent a tragic choking. Do not let young children play with toys small enough to fit into their mouths, such as uninflated balloons, marbles and small toy soldiers. Cut the child's food into very small pieces before serving it. And do not offer dangerous foods, including grapes, peanuts, popcorn, hard candy, chewing gum and hot dogs.

If despite these precautions a child does start to choke, think before you act. If the child can talk or cough, he is getting enough air to breathe and should be left alone: Coughing is the best remedy for choking. Do not pound him on the back, because that might just push the object further down.

But if the child cannot make a sound, turns blue and grabs his throat, you must intervene immediately. The proper technique depends on the child's age: An infant under 12 months old requires a special, gentle technique *(top)*, while an older child can be treated almost like an adult *(bottom)*.

If your first attempts do not expel the obstruction, quickly call the rescue squad. But then immediately resume work on the choking child while waiting for help to arrive. Continue even if he loses consciousness, because that often relaxes the muscles and allows you to dislodge the object from the windpipe. The key to success is to keep steadily trying. If the obstruction remains after 60 seconds of unconsciousness, start mouth-to-mouth resuscitation.

Caution: The emergency first-aid instructions on these pages are not meant to substitute for formal training in first-aid techniques. To be fully prepared to handle accidents and medical emergencies, you should take a course in first aid and in cardiopulmonary resuscitation (CPR). Call your local hospital or Red Cross chapter to find out how you can enroll in such a course.

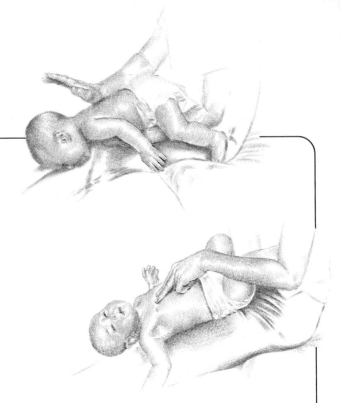

To clear the windpipe of a child under 12 months old, hold the baby face down on your lap as shown (top). With the heel of your hand strike four sharp blows between the shoulder blades. If choking continues, turn the baby over. Put two or three fingertips on his breastbone (above) and quickly press four times, depressing the breastbone about ½ inch. Alternate between back blows and chest compressions until the object obstructing breathing is dislodged.

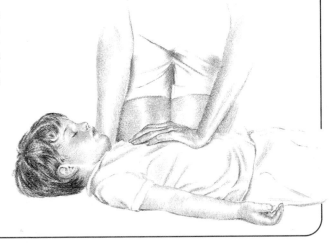

To help a choking child more than one year old, lay the child on the floor, face up. Put the heel of your hand midway between his navel and rib cage (above). Give six to 10 sharp, rapid thrusts upward toward the child's shoulder blades. Then open the child's mouth; if the object is visible, remove it. Otherwise repeat the abdominal thrusts until the object is forced out.

Bibliography

BOOKS

Adolf, Barbara, and Karol Rose, *The Employer's Guide to Child Care*. New York: Praeger, 1985.

Ashery, Rebecca Sager, and Michele Margolin Basen, *The Parents with Careers Workbook*. Washington: Acropolis Books, 1983.

Auerbach, Stevanne:
Choosing Child Care: A Guide for Parents. New York: E. P. Dutton, 1981.
The Whole Child: A Sourcebook. New York: Perigee Books, 1981.

Bank Street College of Education, *The Pleasure of Their Company: How to Have More Fun with Your Children*. Radnor, Pa.: Chilton Book Company, 1981.

Benton, Barbara, *The Babysitter's Handbook*. New York: William Morrow and Company, 1981.

Berg, Barbara J., *The Crisis of the Working Mother: Resolving the Conflict Between Family and Work*. New York: Summit Books, 1986.

Bowlby, John, M.D., *Maternal Care and Mental Health*. Geneva: World Health Organization, 1951.

Brazelton, T. Berry, M.D., *Working and Caring*. Reading, Mass.: Addison-Wesley, 1985.

Burck, Frances Wells, *Baby Sense: A Practical and Supportive Guide to Baby Care*. New York: St. Martin's Press, 1979.

Caplan, Frank, and Theresa Caplan, *The Power of Play*. Garden City, N.Y.: Anchor Press/Doubleday, 1973.

Childhood Medical Guide, by the Editors of Time-Life Books (Successful Parenting series). Alexandria, Va.: Time-Life Books, 1986.

Clarke-Stewart, Alison, *Daycare*. Cambridge: Harvard University Press, 1982.

Collins, Alice H., and Eunice L. Watson, *Family Day Care: A Practical Guide for Parents, Caregivers, and Professionals*. Boston: Beacon Press, 1976.

Dodson, Fitzhugh, *How to Father*. Los Angeles: Nash Publishing, 1974.

Eagan, Andrea Boroff, *The Newborn Mother: Stages of Her Growth*. Boston: Little, Brown & Co., 1985.

Eichenberger, Shirley, *Mother's Day Out: How to Start a Business That Gives Mothers the Day Off*. Overland Park, Kans.: Oak Hill Publishers, 1983.

Endsley, Richard C., and Marilyn R. Bradbard, *Quality Day Care: A Handbook of Choices for Parents and Caregivers*. Englewood Cliffs, N.J.: Prentice-Hall, 1981.

Filstrup, Jane Merrill, and Dorothy W. Gross, *Monday through Friday: Day Care Alternatives*. New York: Teachers College Press, 1982.

Fish, Debra, *Home-Based Training Resource Handbook*. St. Paul: Toys 'n Things Training and Resource Center, 1980.

Goetz, Elizabeth M., and K. Eileen Allen, *Early Childhood Education: Special Environmental, Policy, and Legal Considerations*. Rockville, Md.: Aspen Systems Corporation, 1983.

Gordon, Ira J., *Baby Learning through Baby Play: A Parent's Guide for the First Two Years*. New York: St. Martin's Press, 1970.

Grad, Rae, et al., *The Father Book: Pregnancy and Beyond*. Washington: Acropolis Books, 1981.

Grollman, Earl A., and Gerri L. Sweder, *The Working Parent Dilemma*. Boston: Beacon Press, 1986.

Gunzenhauser, Nina, and Bettye M. Caldwell, eds., *Group Care for Young Children: Considerations for Child Care and Health Professionals, Public Policy Makers and Parents*. Somerville, N.J.: Johnson & Johnson, 1986.

Highberger, Ruth, *Child Development for Day Care Workers*. Boston: Houghton Mifflin, 1976.

Howe, Louise Kapp, ed., *The Future of the Family*. New York: Simon and Schuster, 1972.

James, Elizabeth, and Carol Barkin, *The Complete Babysitter's Handbook*. New York: Julian Messner, 1980.

Kamerman, Sheila B., and Cheryl D. Hayes, eds., *Families That Work: Children in a Changing World*. Washington: National Academy Press, 1982.

Kappelman, Murray M., M.D., and Paul R. Ackerman, *Parents After Thirty*. New York: Rawson, Wade Publishers, 1980.

Kelly, Marguerite, and Elia Parsons, *The Mother's Almanac*. Garden City, N.Y.: Doubleday, 1975.

Kiester, Edwin, Jr., Sally Valente Kiester and the Editors of Better Homes and Gardens Books, *New Baby Book*. Des Moines, Iowa: Meredith Corporation, 1985.

Kuzma, Kay, *Working Mothers: How You Can Have a Career and Be a Good Parent, Too*. Los Angeles: Stratford Press, 1981.

Langenbach, Michael, *Day Care: Curriculum Considerations*. Columbus, Ohio: Charles E. Merrill, 1977.

Lansky, Vicki, *Dear Babysitter*. Deephaven, Minn.: Meadowbrook, Inc., 1982.

Leavitt, Robin Lynn, and Brenda Krause Eheart, *Toddler Day Care: A Guide to Responsive Caregiving*. Lexington, Mass.: Lexington Books, 1985.

Lowndes, Marion, *A Manual for Baby-Sitters*. Boston: Little, Brown & Co., 1974.

Madden, Chris Casson, *Baby Hints*. New York: Fawcett Columbine, 1982.

Marzollo, Jean, *Supertot: Creative Learning Activities for Children from One to Three and Sympathetic Advice for Their Parents*. New York: Harper Colophon Books, 1977.

Mayer, Gloria Gilbert, *2001 Hints for Working Mothers*. New York: Quill, 1983.

Maynard, Fredelle, *The Child Care Crisis: The Real Costs of Day Care for You — and Your Child*. New York: Viking, 1985.

Meyers, Carole Terwilliger, *How to Organize a Babysitting Cooperative and Get Some Free Time Away from the Kids*. Albany, Calif.: Carousel Press, 1976.

Mitchell, Grace, *The Day Care Book: A Guide for Working Parents to Help Them Find the Best Possible Day Care for Their Children*. New York: Fawcett Columbine, 1979.

Norris, Gloria, and Jo Ann Miller, *The Working Mother's Complete Handbook*. New York: New American Library, 1984.

Olds, Sally Wendkos, *The Working Parents Survival Guide*. Toronto: Bantam, 1983.

Parke, Ross D., *Fathers*. Cambridge: Harvard University Press, 1981.

Piers, Maria W., ed., *Play and Development*. New York: W. W. Norton & Co., 1972.

Pizzo, Peggy, *Parent to Parent: Working Together for Ourselves and Our Children*. Boston: Beacon Press, 1983.

Provence, Sally, M.D., *Guide for the Care of Infants in Groups*. New York: Child Welfare League of America, 1967.

Provence, Sally, M.D., Audrey Naylor and June Patterson, *The Challenge of Daycare*. New Haven, Conn.: Yale University Press, 1977.

Ross, Kathy Gallagher, *A Parents' Guide to Day Care: Finding the Best Alternative for Your Child*. Vancouver, B.C.: International Self-Counsel Press, Ltd., 1984.

Rozdilsky, Mary Lou, and Barbara Banet, *What Now? A Handbook for New Parents*. New York: Charles Scribner's Sons, 1972.

Salk, Lee, *The Complete Dr. Salk: An A-to-Z Guide to Raising Your Child*. New York: New American Library, 1983.

Scharlatt, Elisabeth L., ed., *Kids: Day In and Day Out*. New York: Simon and Schuster, 1979.

Schiller, Judith D., *Child-Care Alternatives and Emotional Well-Being*. New York: Praeger, 1980.

Siegel-Gorelick, Bryna, *The Working Parents' Guide to Child Care*. Boston: Little, Brown & Co., 1983.

Sills, Barbara, and Jeanne Henry, *The Mother to Mother Baby Care Book*. New York: Avon, 1980.

Skolnick, Arlene S., and Jerome H. Skolnick, *Family in Transition: Rethinking Marriage, Sexuality, Child Rearing, and Family Organization*. Boston: Little, Brown & Co., 1983.

Spizman, Robyn Freedman, *Lollipop Grapes and Clothespin Critters*. Reading, Mass.: Addison-Wesley, 1985.

Squibb, Betsy, *Family Day Care: How to Provide It in Your Home*. Boston: Harvard Common Press, 1980.

Suransky, Valerie Polakow, *The Erosion of Childhood*. Chicago: University of Chicago Press, 1982.

Touw, Kathleen, *Parent Tricks-of-the-Trade*.

Washington: Acropolis Books, 1981.

Wolf, Dennie Palmer, ed., *Connecting: Friendship in the Lives of Young Children and Their Teachers.* Redmond, Wash.: Exchange Press, 1986.

Zigler, Edward F., and Edmund W. Gordon, eds. *Day Care: Scientific and Social Policy Issues.* Boston: Auburn House Publishing Company, 1982.

PERIODICALS

"American Baby Basics #7: What You Need to Know About Child-Care Alternatives." *American Baby,* July 1986.

Caldwell, Bettye M.:

"Day Care and the Public Schools — Natural Allies, Natural Enemies." *Educational Leadership,* February 1986.

"The Trickiest Triangle." *Working Mother,* April 1986.

"What's So Special about Toddlers?" *Working Mother,* June 1985.

Campagna, Vicki, "How to Find a Super Sitter." *Baby Talk,* February 1986.

Crohn, Helen:

"How to Make the Sitter Do Things Your Way." *Working Mother,* September 1983.

"When and How to Fire the Babysitter." *Working Mother,* May 1983.

Crout, Teresa Kochmar, "Finding a Sitter." *Baby Talk,* November 1984.

Fasciano, Nancy, "From Wheezles and Sneezles to Chicken Soup." *Working Mother,* October 1985.

Galinsky, Ellen, "What Really Constitutes Quality Care?" *Exchange,* September 1986.

Gaylin, Jody, "Vacation without Baby." *Parents,* April 1983.

Gibson, Janice T., "Selecting a Babysitter." *Parents,* November 1985.

Greenspan, Stanley I., M.D., and Nancy Thorndike Greenspan, "Where Did Mrs. Davis Go?" *Working Mother,* May 1983.

Gregg, Gail, "Putting Kids First." *New York Times Magazine,* April 13, 1986.

Haac, Linda A., "Report on Day Care and Illness." *Developments from the Child Development Institute of the University of North Carolina at Chapel Hill,* Summer 1986.

Haskins, Ron, and Jonathan Kotch, M.D., "Day Care and Illness: Evidence, Costs, and Public Policy." *Pediatrics,* Supplement, June 1986.

Katz, Lilian G., "Care-Giver Relations." *Parents,* January 1985.

Kelly, Kate, "When You're the Boss." *Mother Today,* July/August 1983.

Kunz, Kathleen, "In-Home Help." *Mothers Today,* September/October 1986.

Lansky, Vicki, "How to Search for a Real-Life Mary Poppins." *Baby Talk,* July 1983.

McCall, Robert B., "Preparing for a Babysitter." *Parents,* December 1984.

McKean, Kevin, and Pamela Ramsey McKean, "Smart Strategies for Finding the Best Sitter." *Working Mother,* October 1986.

Mason, Brook, "Help! How to Find It, Keep It, Manage It, and How Much to Pay." *Child,* October 1986.

Miller, Lisa, "Hiring a Competent Sitter." *Mother Today,* September/October 1983.

Nyros, Marilyn, "Newborns in Day Care Present Very Special Concerns to the Working Mother." *Baby Talk,* June 1985.

Pomeranz, Virginia E., M.D., and Dodi Schultz, "About Babysitters." *Parents,* February 1985.

Shannon, Salley, "Searching for Good Child Care." *Washingtonian,* October 1986.

Squires, Sally, "It's Not Just Measles Anymore." *American Health,* September 1986.

Sullivan, Marguerite Hoxie, "Childcare." *Washington Woman,* May 1984.

Theroux, Phyllis, "Let's Get Away from Them All." *Parents,* July 1986.

OTHER PUBLICATIONS

"Accreditation Criteria and Procedures." Position statement of the National Academy of Early Childhood Programs. Washington: National Association for the Education of Young Children, 1984.

"Child and Dependent Care Credit, and Employment Taxes for Household Employers." Publication 503. Washington: Department of the Treasury, Internal Revenue Service, November 1985.

Friedman, David B., June S. Sale and Vivian Weinstein, *Child Care and the Family.* Chicago: National Committee for Prevention of Child Abuse, 1984.

"A Parent's Guide to Day Care." DHHS Publication No. (OHDS) 80-30254. Washington: U.S. Department of Health and Human Services, March 1980.

"The Pocket Guide to Babysitting." DHHS Publication No. (OHDS) 80-30045. Washington: U.S. Department of Health and Human Services, 1980.

Spelman, Cornelia, *Talking about Child Sexual Abuse.* Chicago: National Committee for Prevention of Child Abuse, 1985.

U.S. Consumer Product Safety Commission, "The Super Sitter." Washington: September 1983.

"What You Can Do to Stop Disease in the Child Day Care Center: A Handbook for Caregivers." Washington: Department of Health and Human Services, December 1984.

"What You Can Do to Stop Disease in Your Child's Day Care Center: A Handbook for Parents." Washington: Department of Health and Human Services, December 1984.

"Women Who Maintain Families." Fact Sheet No. 86-2. Washington: U.S. Department of Labor Women's Bureau, 1986.

"Working Mothers and Their Children." Fact Sheet No. 85-4. Washington: U.S. Department of Labor Women's Bureau, July 1985.

Acknowledgments and Picture Credits

The index for this book was prepared by Louise Hedberg. The editors also thank: Susan Blair, Alexandria, Va.; Helen Blank, Children's Defense Fund, Washington; Mary Boss, Madison, Wis.; Michael Coleman, Falls Church, Va.; Susan Devaney, New York; Judie Fien-Helfman, Washington; Jane Goodrich, Madison, Wis.; Ron Haskins, M.D., U.S. House of Representatives, Washington; Susan Hilbert, Annandale, Va.; Alice Sterling Honig, M.D., Syracuse University, Syracuse, N.Y.; Amy Killeen, M.D., Frederick, Md.; Elaine M. McEnteggart, New York; Carol Mickey, Washington; Old Towne Child Development Center, Alexandria, Va.; Margaret Palmquist, Fairfax, Va.; Melissa Reed, Madison, Wis.; Patricia Spahr, The National Association for the Education of Young Children, Washington; Suzanne Szasz, New York; Mary Jane Thompson, Deerfield, Ill.; Elaine Traite, Burke, Va.; T. Vandover, Fairfax, Va.; Julie Walsh, Madison, Wis.; Sue Werner, Madison, Wis.; Barbara Willer, The National Association for the Education of Young Children, Washington; Deborah Wills, Arlington, Va.; Barbara Worthington, Madison, Wis.

The sources for the photographs in this book are listed below, followed by the sources for the illustrations. Credits from left to right are separated by semicolons; credits from top to bottom are separated by dashes.

Photographs. Cover: Susie Fitzhugh. 7-19: Neil Kagan. 23: Steven Biver. 25-53: Neil Kagan. 69: Joe Rubino. 79: Beecie Kupersmith. 93: Suzanne Szasz. 103: Willa Zakin. 107: Joe Rubino.

Illustrations. 9: Paine, Bluett, Paine. Inc. 11-15: Donald Gates from photos by Neil Kagan. 29-55: Kathe Scherr from photos by Neil Kagan. 59: Kathe Scherr from photo by Eliot Marshall. 61-67: Kathe Scherr from photos by Neil Kagan. 70, 71: Marguerite E. Bell from photos by Neil Kagan. 76: Marguerite E. Bell from photo by Beecie Kupersmith. 77: Marguerite E. Bell from photos by Beecie Kupersmith and Myrna Traylor-Herndon. 80-85: Marguerite E. Bell from photos by Beecie Kupersmith. 90, 91: Marguerite E. Bell from photos by Carolyn Rothery and Myrna Traylor-Herndon. 95-99: Marguerite E. Bell from photos by Neil Kagan. 101: Gail Prensky. 110-113: Robert Hynes from photos by Beecie Kupersmith. 114: Robert Hynes from photo by Beecie Kupersmith — Robert Hynes from photo by Cadge Productions/The Image Bank. 115, 116: Robert Hynes from photos by Beecie Kupersmith. 117: Robert Hynes from photo by Susie Fitzhugh. 118-123: Donald Gates from photos by Beecie Kupersmith. 124: Roger Essley from photo by Joe Rubino. 125-127: Roger Essley from photos by Beecie Kupersmith. 128-131: Bill Hennessy from photos by Beecie Kupersmith. 134, 135: Donald Gates from photos by Beecie Kupersmith.

Index